EASY GUITAR
WITH NOTES & TAB

VIDEO GAME MUSIC
FOR GUITAR

ISBN 978-1-5400-5298-8

HAL•LEONARD®

Visit Hal Leonard Online at
www.halleonard.com

Contact us:
Hal Leonard
7777 West Bluemound Road
Milwaukee, WI 53213
Email: info@halleonard.com

In Europe, contact:
Hal Leonard Europe Limited
42 Wigmore Street
Marylebone, London, W1U 2RN
Email: info@halleonardeurope.com

In Australia, contact:
Hal Leonard Australia Pty. Ltd.
4 Lentara Court
Cheltenham, Victoria, 3192 Australia
Email: info@halleonard.com.au

STRUM AND PICK PATTERNS

This chart contains the suggested strum and pick patterns that are referred to by number at the beginning of each song in this book. The symbols ⊓ and ∨ in the strum patterns refer to down and up strokes, respectively. The letters in the pick patterns indicate which right-hand fingers play which strings.

p = thumb
i = index finger
m = middle finger
a = ring finger

For example; Pick Pattern 2
is played: thumb - index - middle - ring

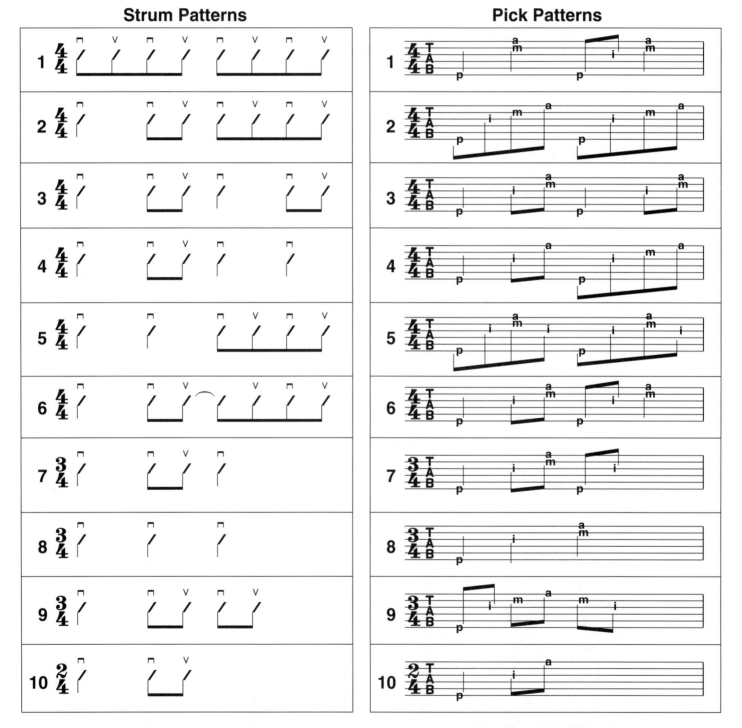

Strum Patterns

Pick Patterns

You can use the 3/4 Strum and Pick Patterns in songs written in compound meter (6/8, 9/8, 12/8, etc.). For example, you can accompany a song in 6/8 by playing the 3/4 pattern twice in each measure. The 4/4 Strum and Pick Patterns can be used for songs written in cut time (¢) by doubling the note time values in the patterns. Each pattern would therefore last two measures in cut time.

Angry Birds Theme

By Ari Pulkkinen

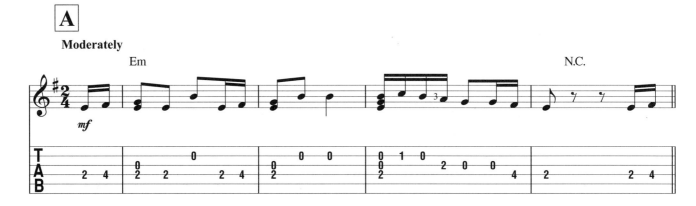

Strum Pattern: 4
Pick Pattern: 3

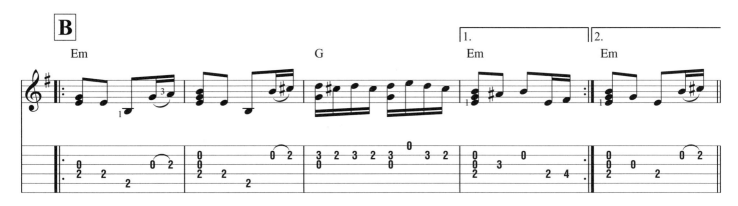

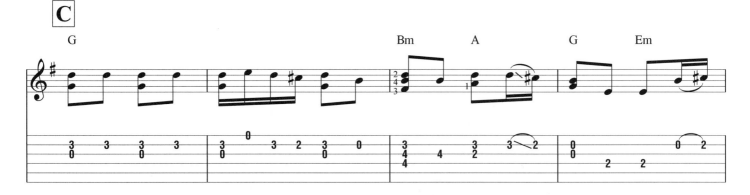

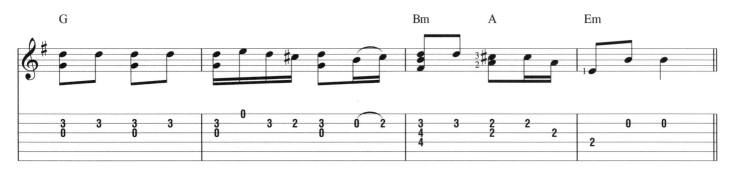

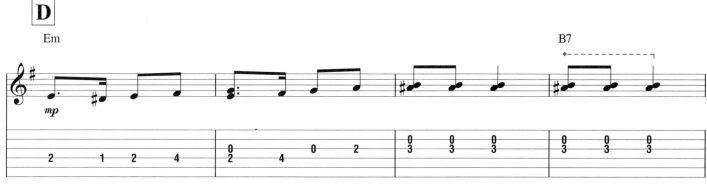

*Optional: Play one octave higher.

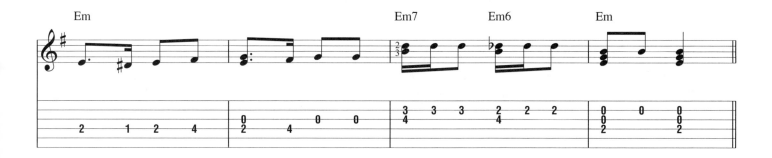

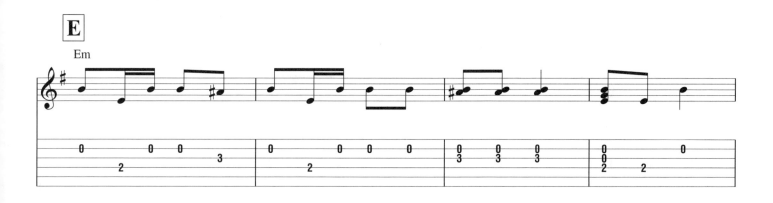

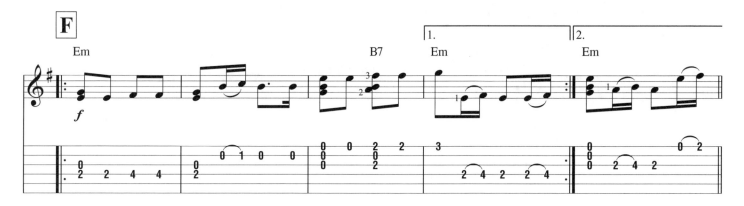

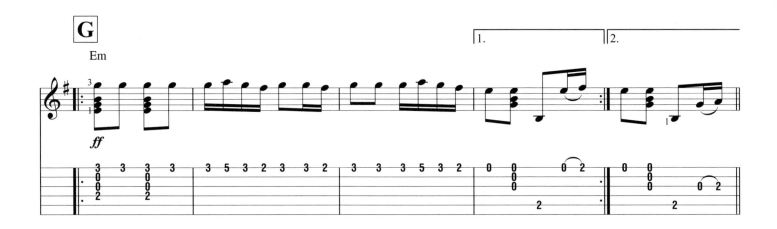

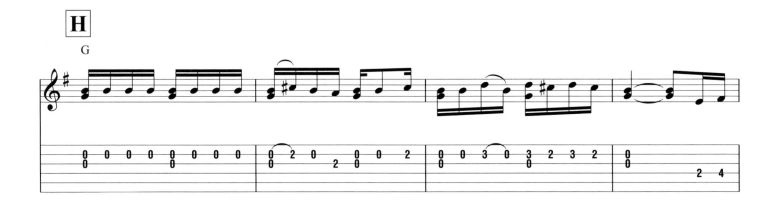

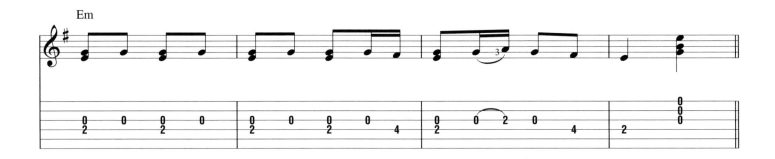

Assassin's Creed III Main Title

By Lorne Balfe

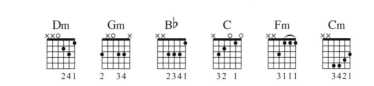

Strum Pattern: 6
Pick Pattern: 4

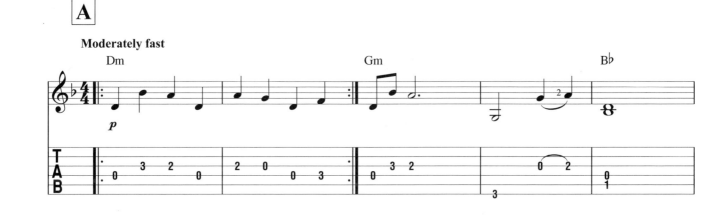

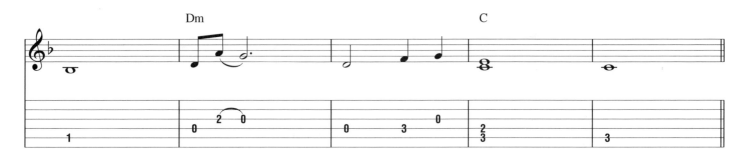

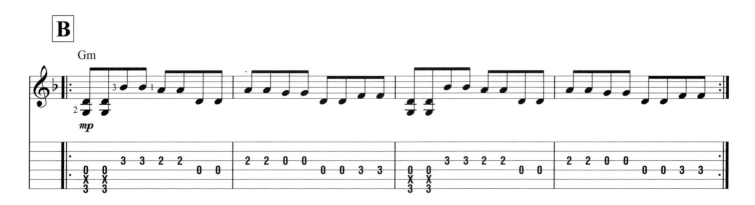

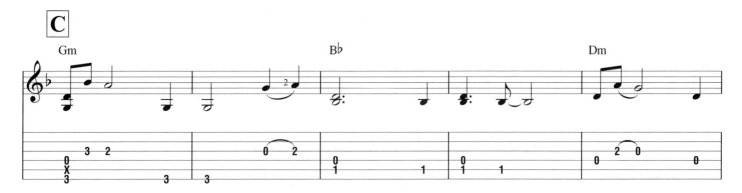

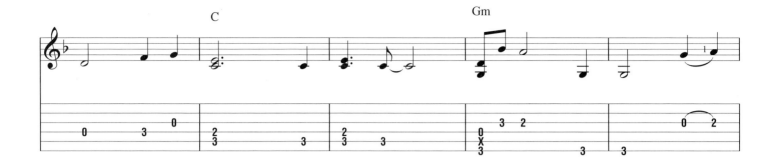

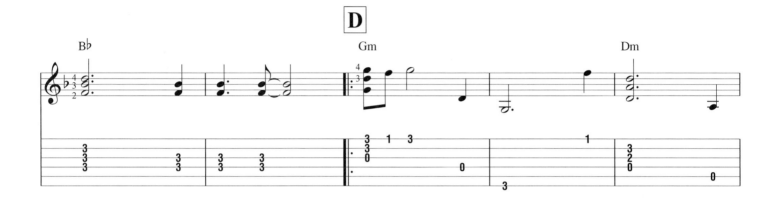

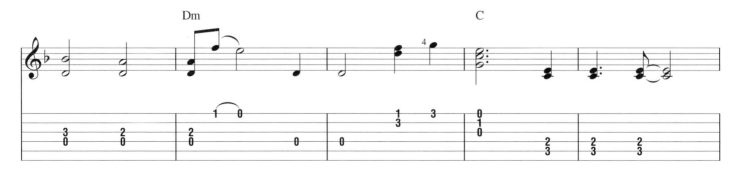

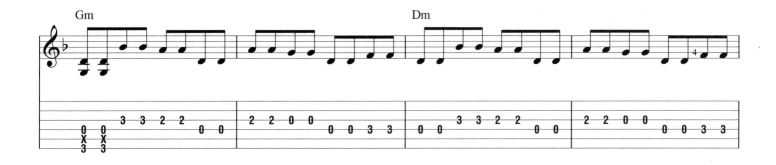

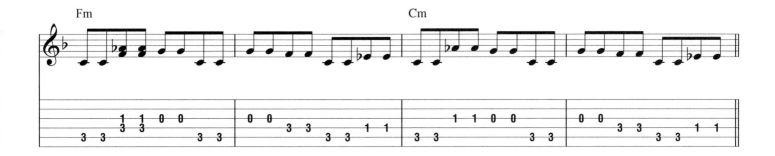

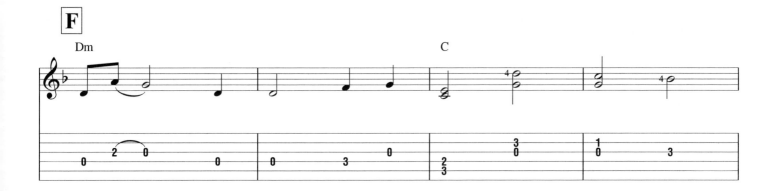

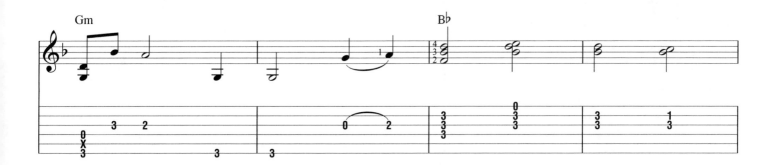

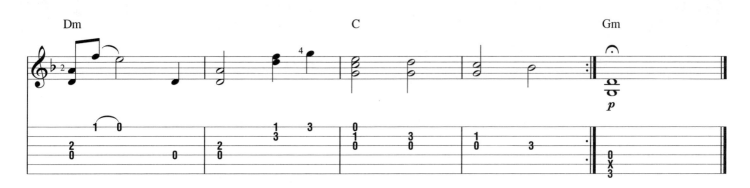

Assassin's Creed Revelations

By Lorne Balfe

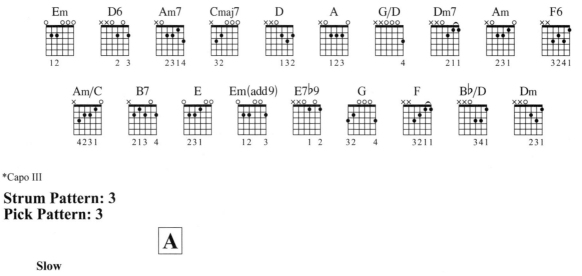

*Capo III

Strum Pattern: 3
Pick Pattern: 3

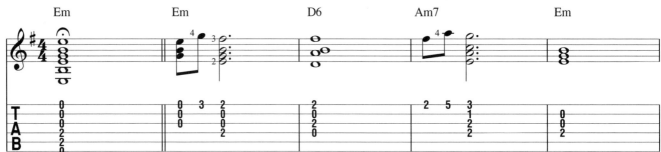

*Optional: To match recording, place capo at 3rd fret.

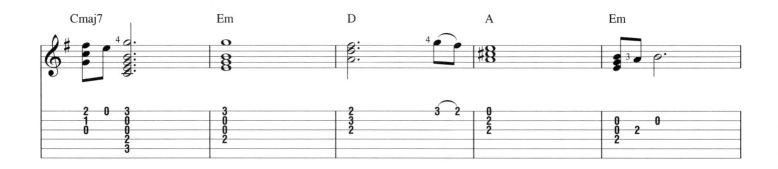

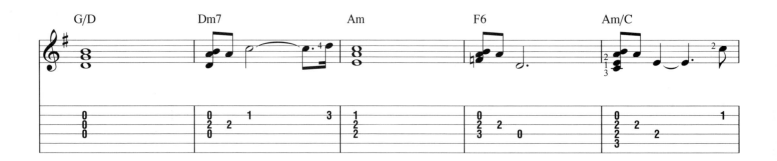

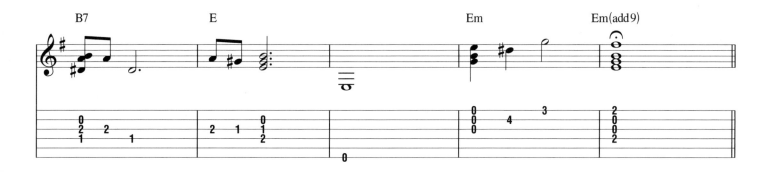

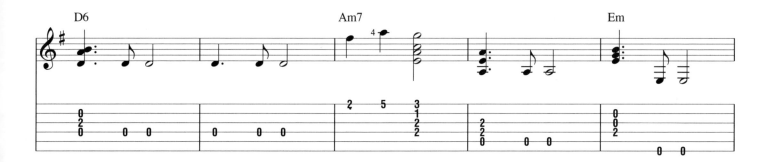

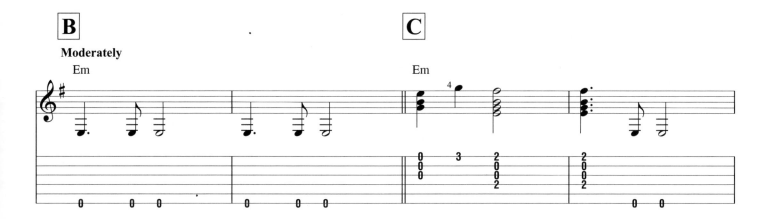

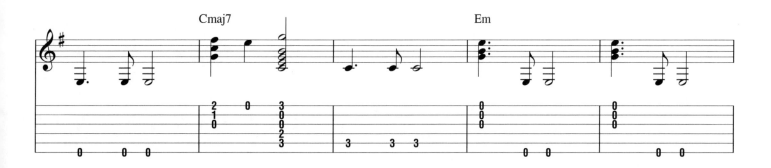

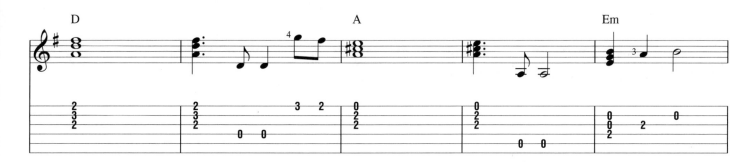

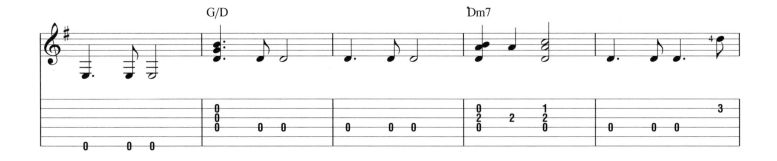

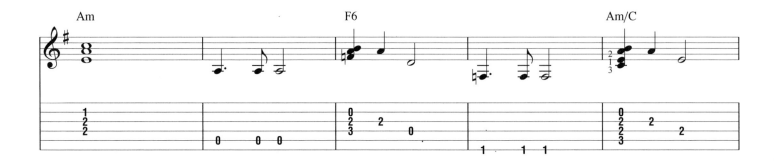

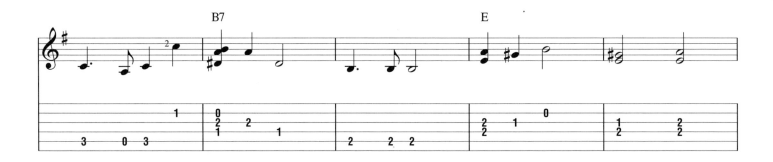

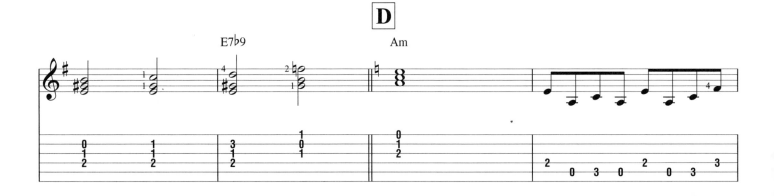

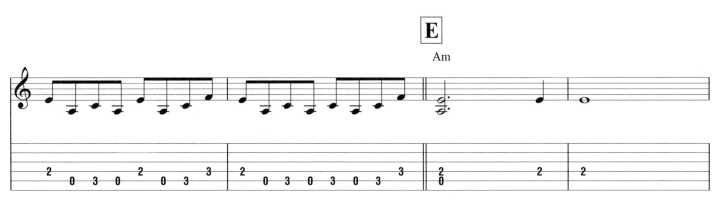

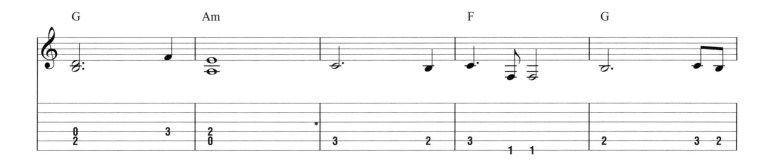

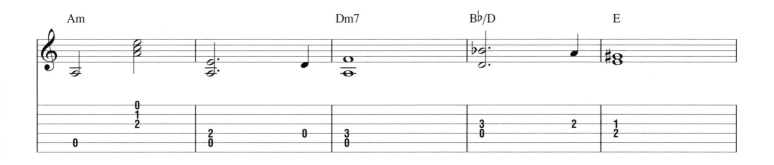

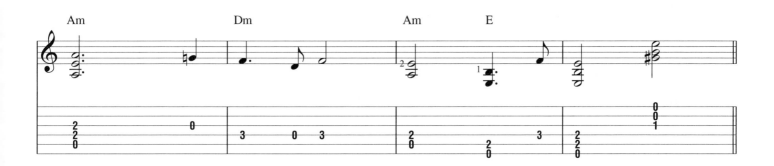

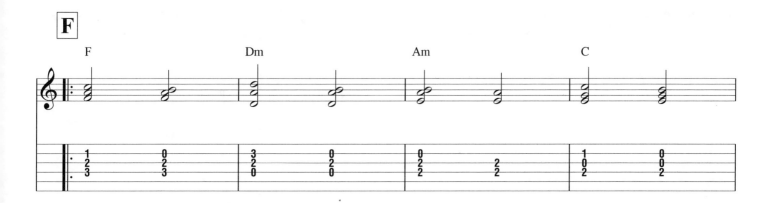

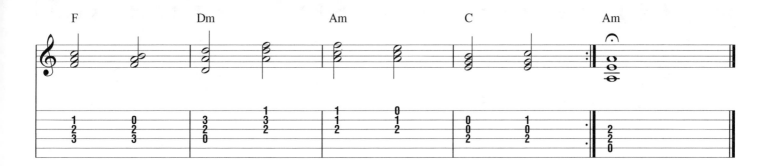

Baba Yetu
from the Video Game CIVILIZATION IV

Words and Music by Christopher Tin

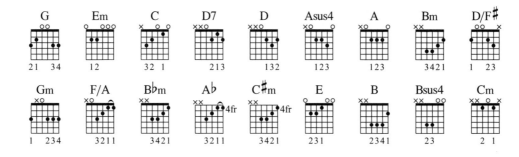

Strum Pattern: 3, 4
Pick Pattern: 2, 5

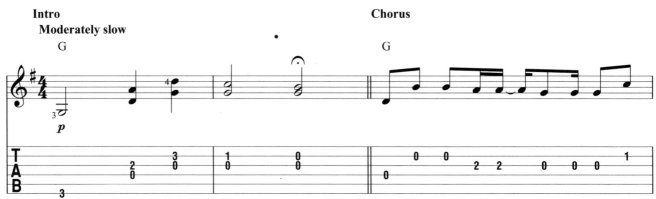

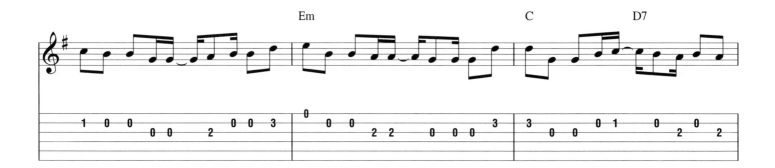

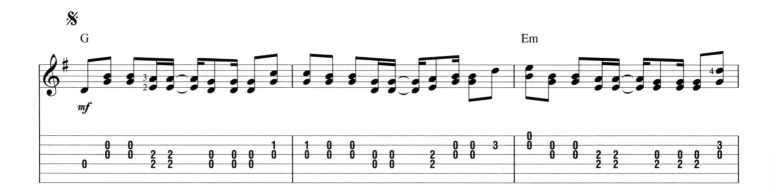

Verse

To Coda ⊕

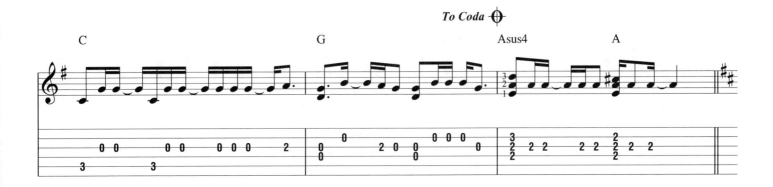

Chorus

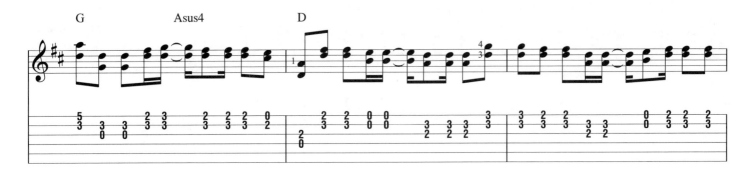

Interlude

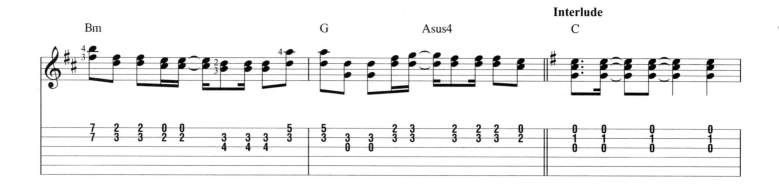

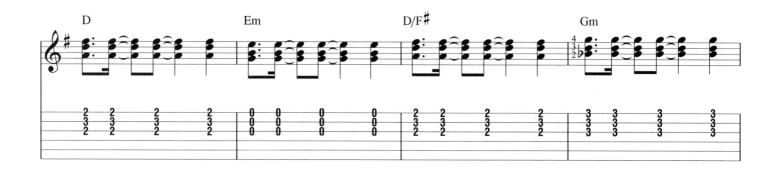

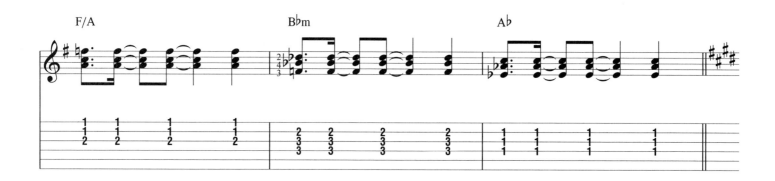

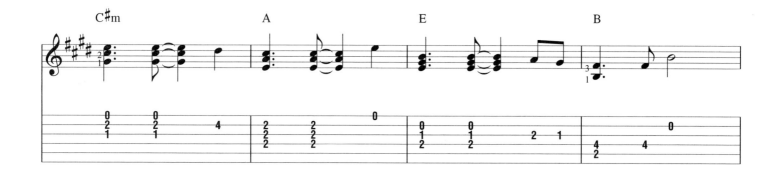

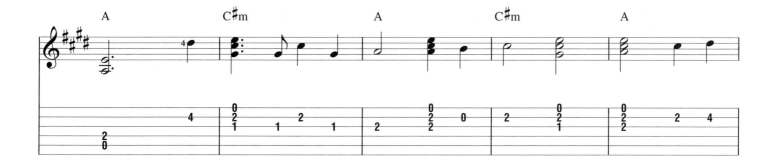

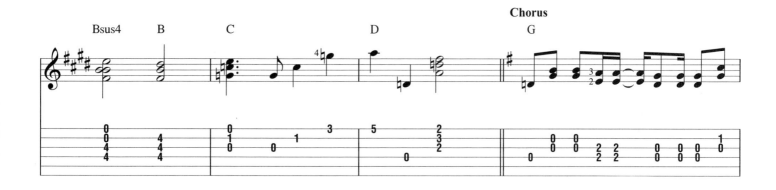

Chorus

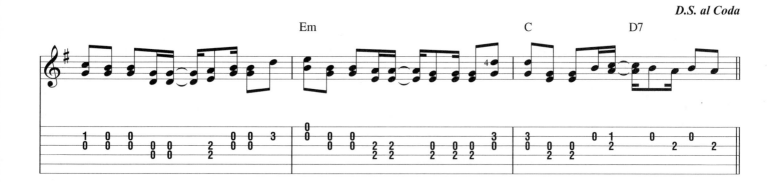

D.S. al Coda

Coda

Outro

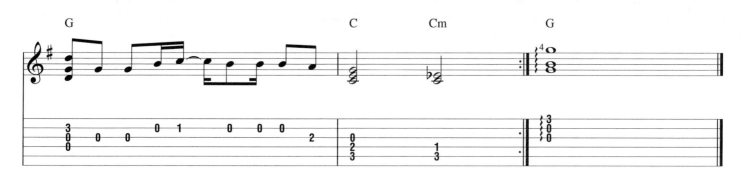

Battlefield 1942
Theme

By Joel Eriksson

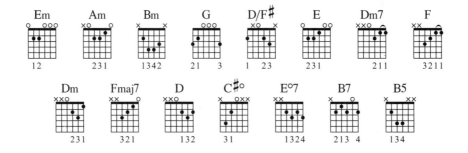

*Capo I

Strum Pattern: 7
Pick Pattern: 7, 8

A

Very fast

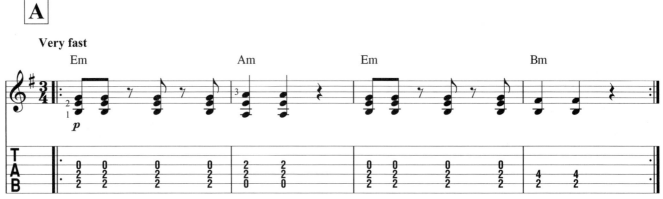

*Optional: To match recording, place capo at 1st fret.

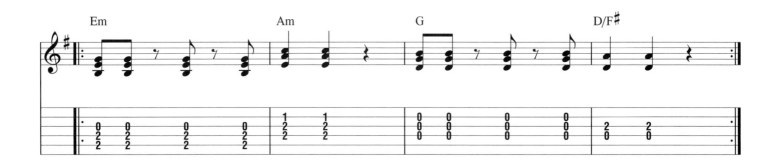

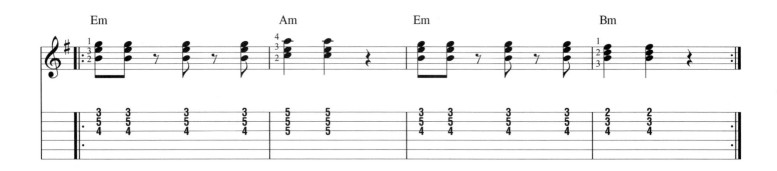

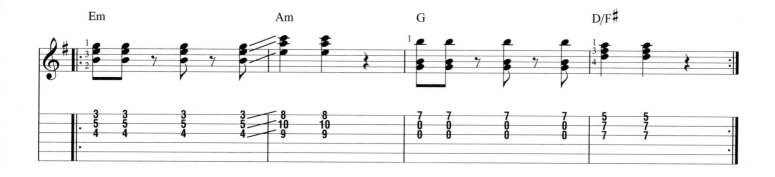

B

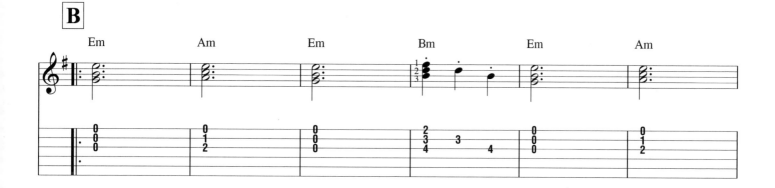

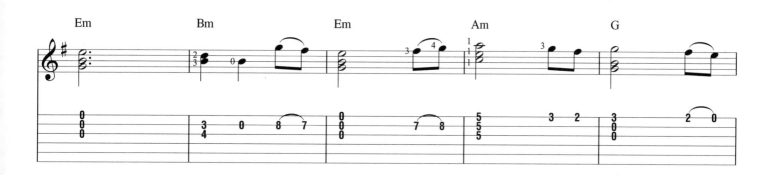

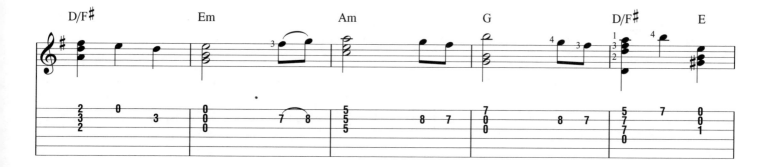

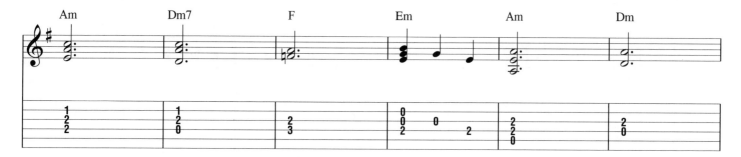

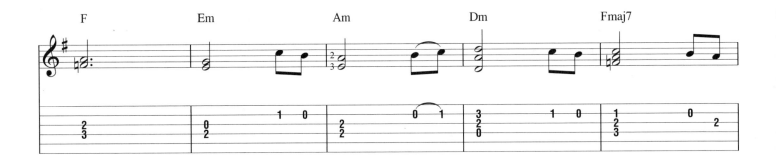

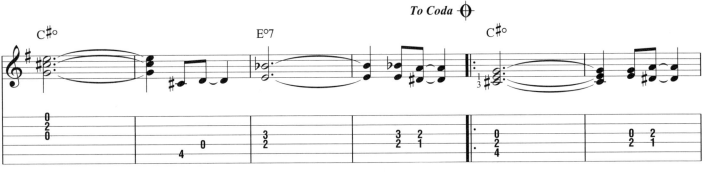

C

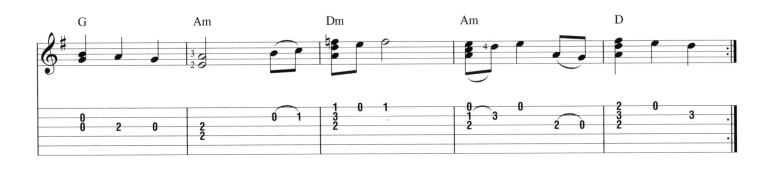

Bounty Hunter

from ADVENT RISING

By Tommy Tallarico

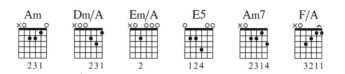

*Capo V

Strum Pattern: 3, 4
Pick Pattern: 1, 3

A

Moderately slow

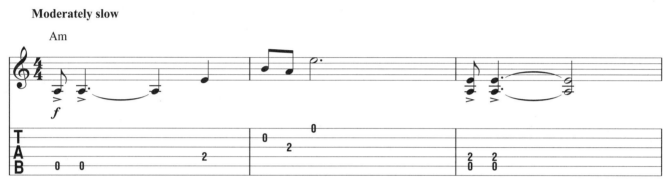

*To match recording, place capo at 5th fret.

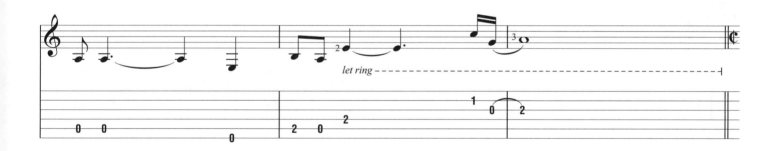

B

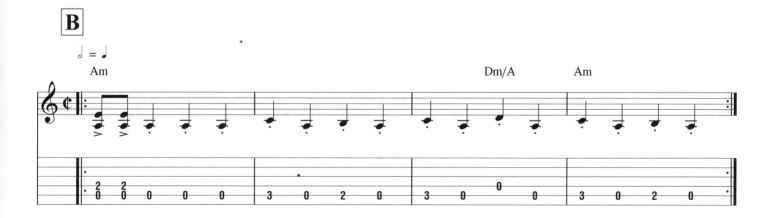

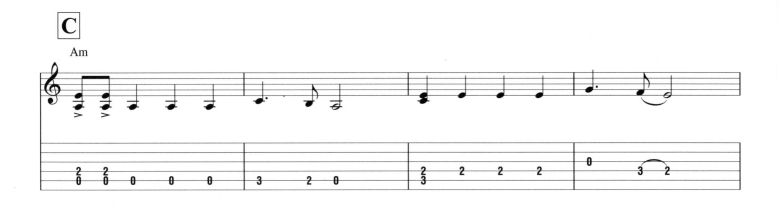

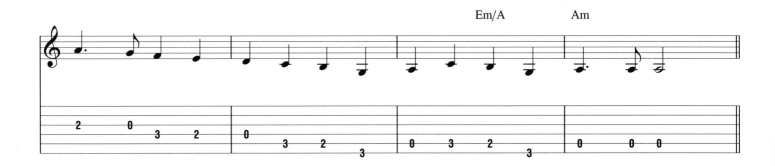

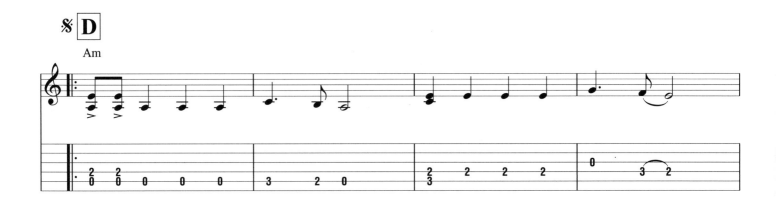

To Coda ⊕

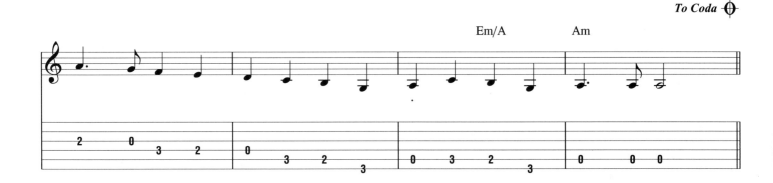

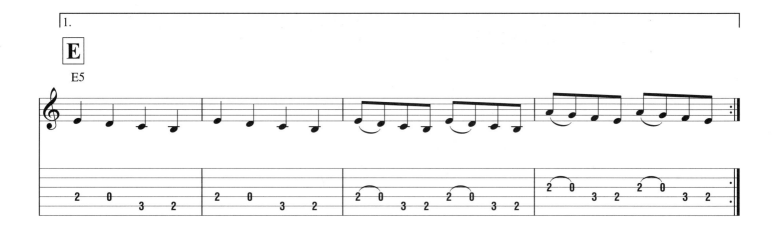

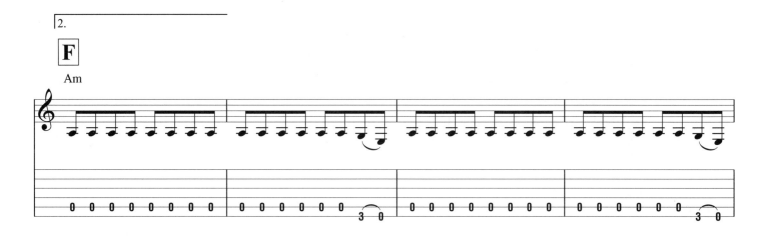

D.S. al Coda

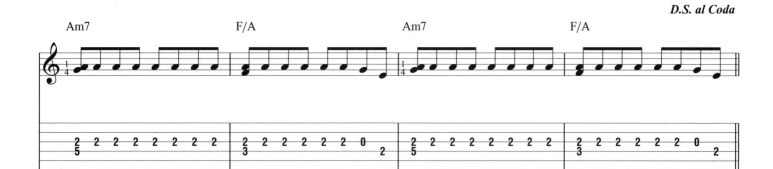

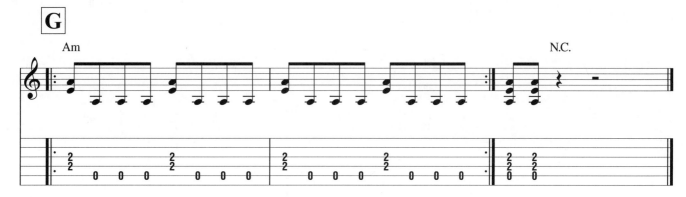

IL-2 Sturmovik: Birds of Prey
Main Theme
By Jeremy Soule

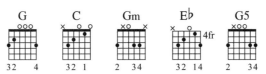

Strum Pattern: 1, 3
Pick Pattern: 1, 2

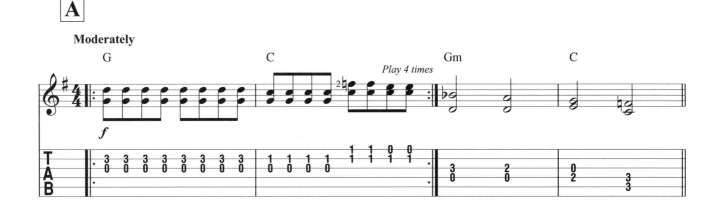

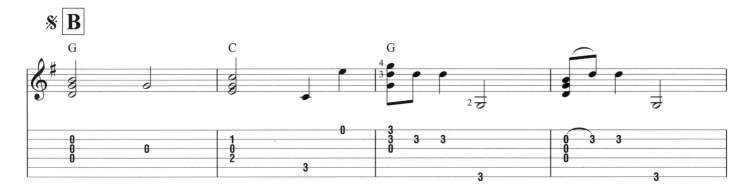

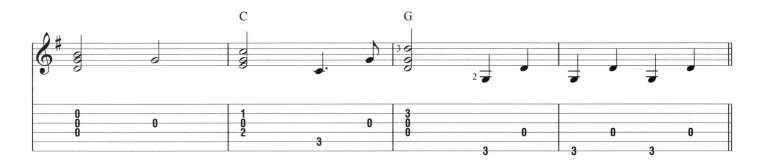

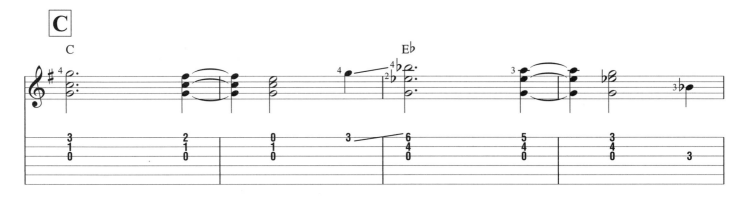

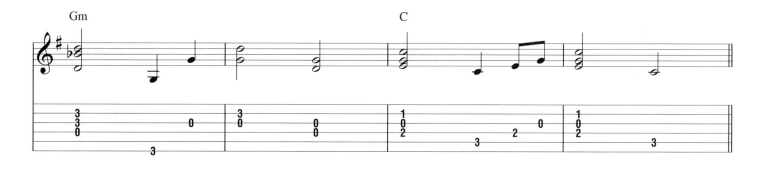

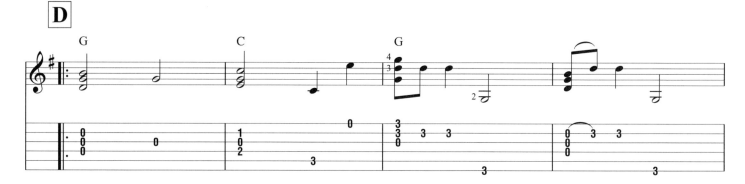

4th time, To Coda ⊕

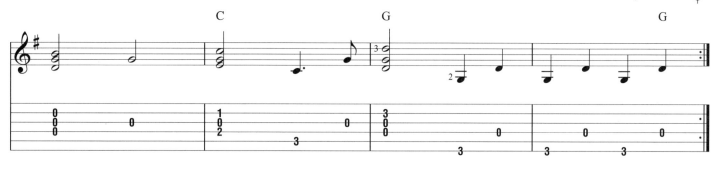

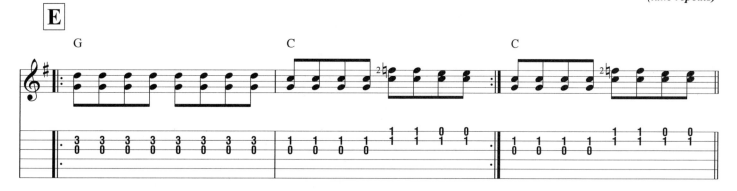

E

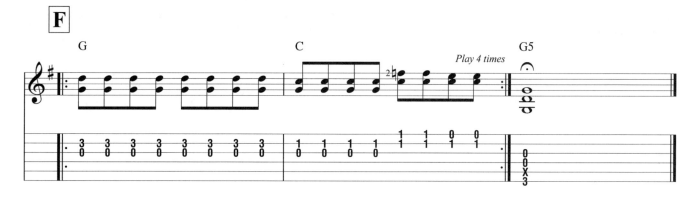

⊕ Coda

F

Bratja
(Brothers)
from FULL METAL ALCHEMIST

Words and Music by Michiru Oshima, Seiji Mizushima and Tatiana Naumova

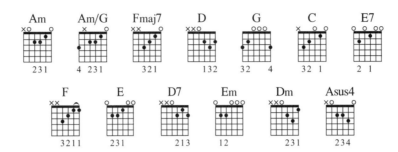

*Capo V

Strum Pattern: 7
Pick Pattern: 9

Moderately fast

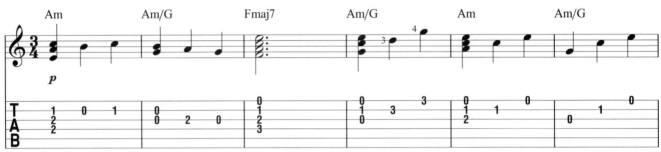

*Optional: To match recording, place capo at 5th fret.

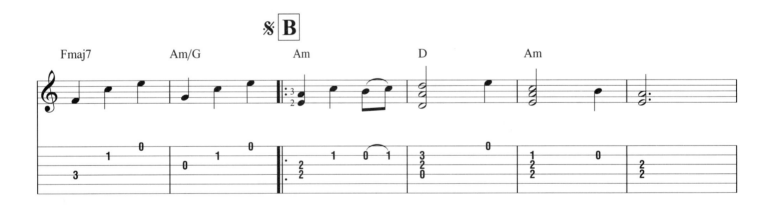

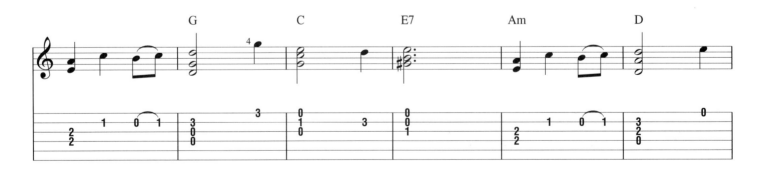

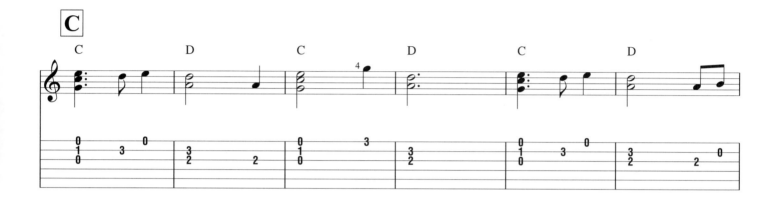

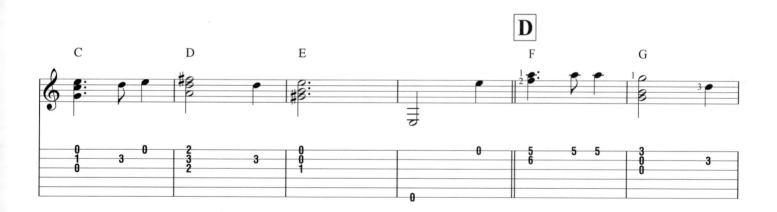

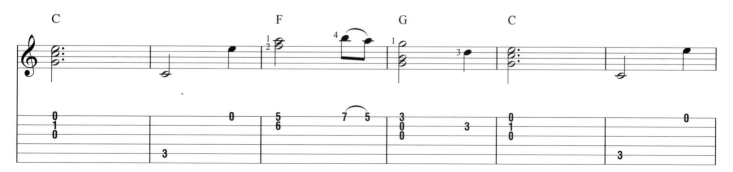

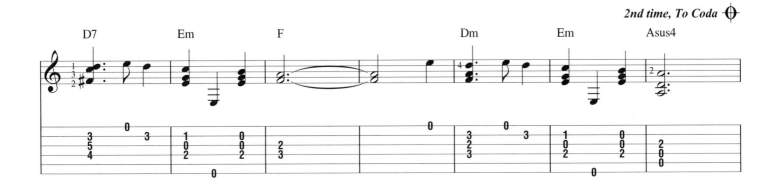

2nd time, To Coda

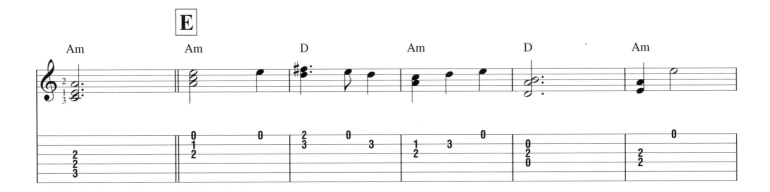

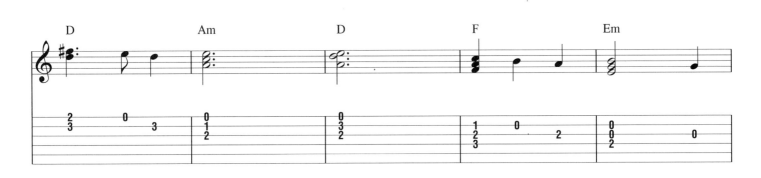

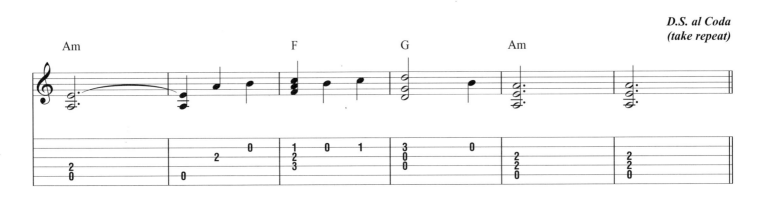

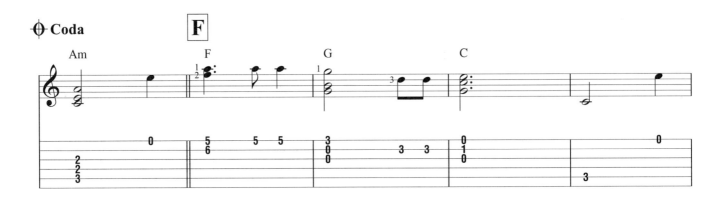

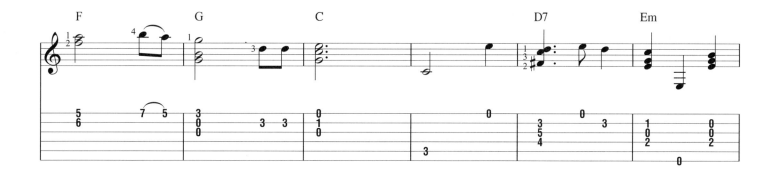

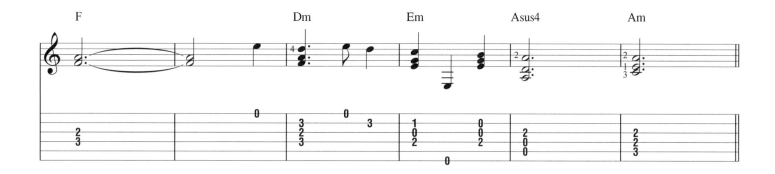

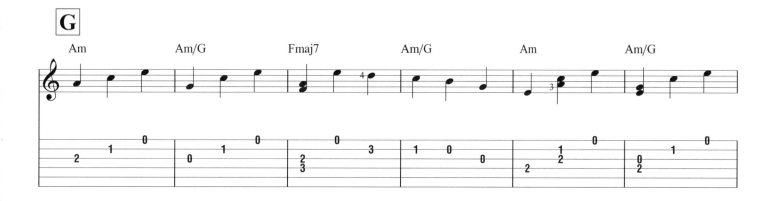

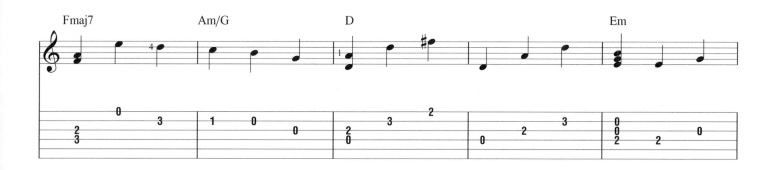

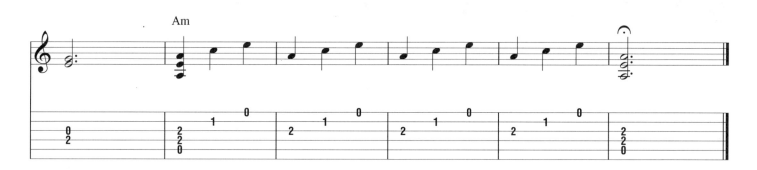

Dearly Beloved

from KINGDOM HEARTS

Music by Yoko Shimomura

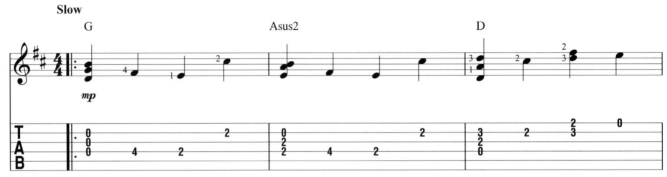

*Capo I

Strum Pattern: 2
Pick Pattern: 2

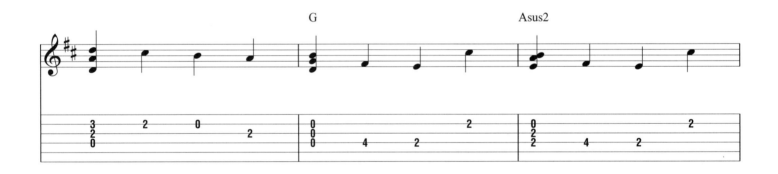

*Optional: To match recording, place capo at 1st fret.

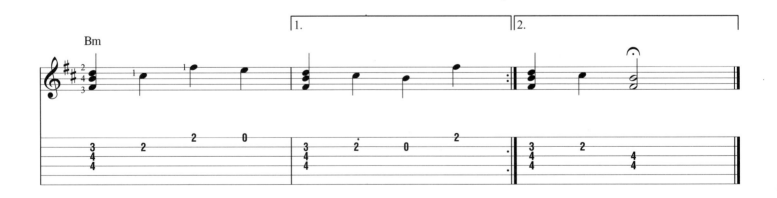

Don't Forget

from DELTARUNE ™

Words and Music by Toby Fox

*Tune down 1/2 step:
(low to high) E♭-A♭-D♭-G♭-B♭-E♭

Strum Pattern: 2, 3
Pick Pattern: 4

Moderately slow, freely

*Optional: To match recording, tune down 1/2 step.

When the light is run-ning low, and the shad-ows start to grow, and the

plac-es that you know seem like fan - ta - sy, _____ there's a light in - side your soul that's still

shin - ing in the cold with the truth, the prom - ise in our hearts. _____

_____ Don't for - get: I'm with you in the dark.

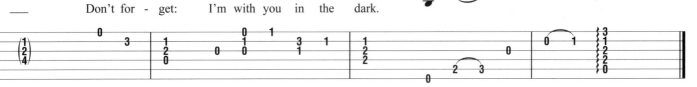

Dragonborn
(Skyrim Theme)

By Jeremy Soule

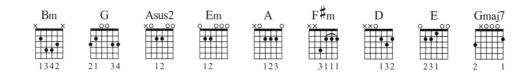

Strum Pattern: 7, 9
Pick Pattern: 7, 8

A

Slowly, in 2

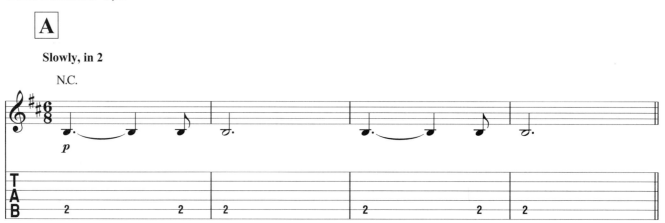

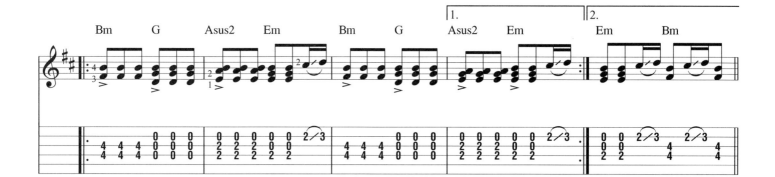

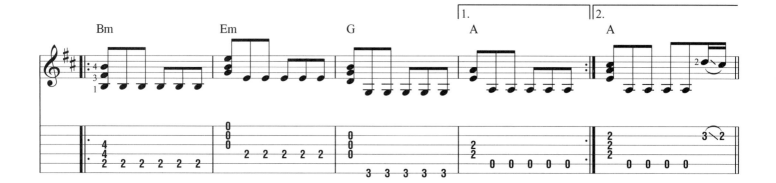

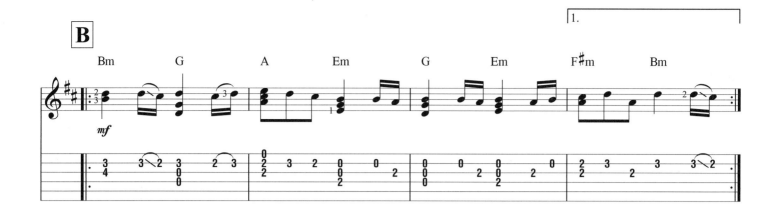

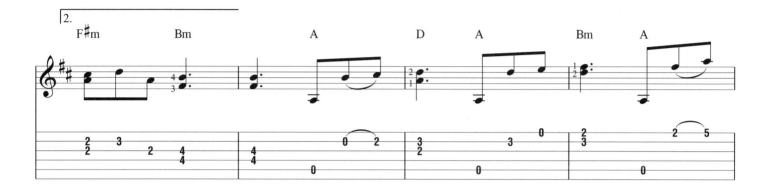

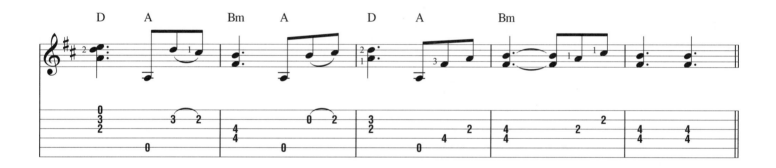

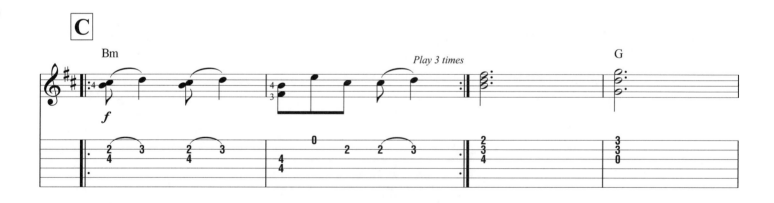

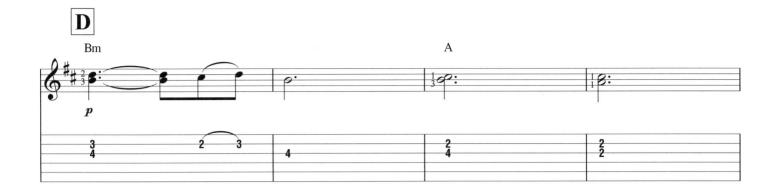

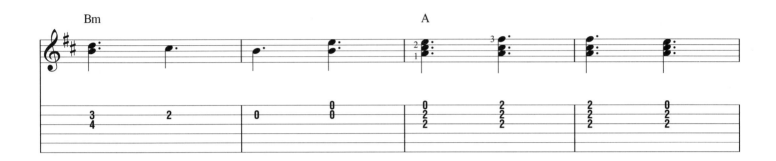

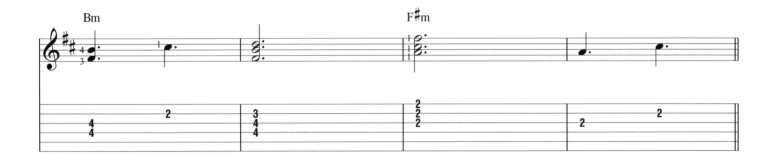

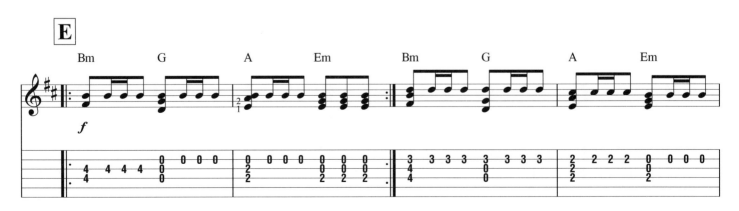

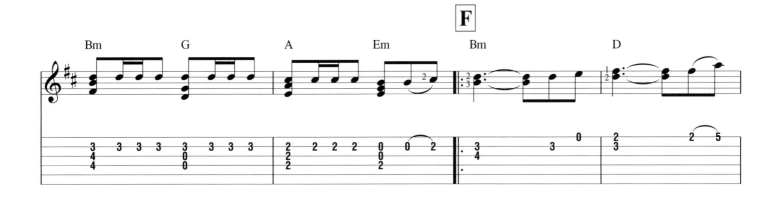

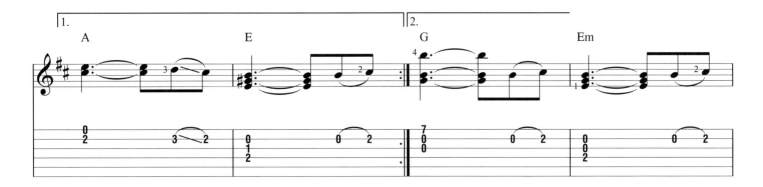

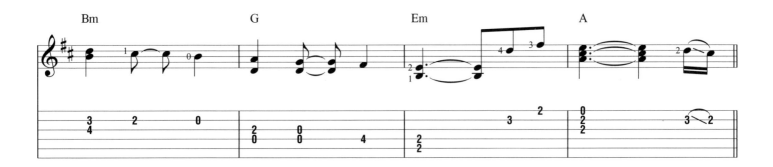

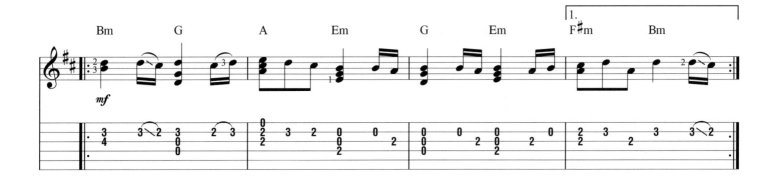

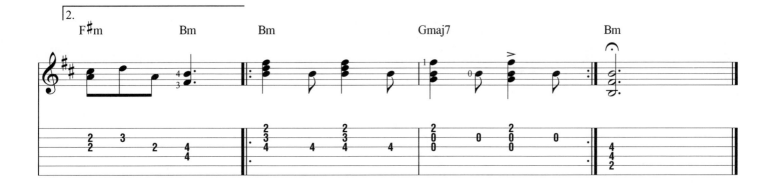

Elder Scrolls: Oblivion

By Jeremy Soule

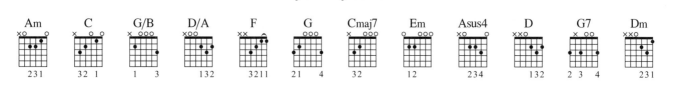

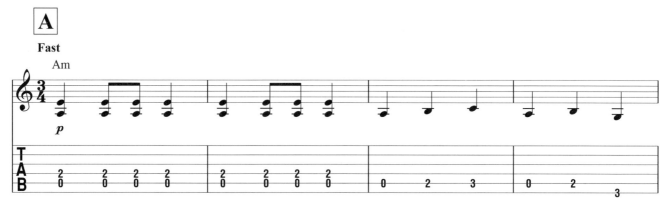

*Capo V

Strum Pattern: 7, 9
Pick Pattern: 7

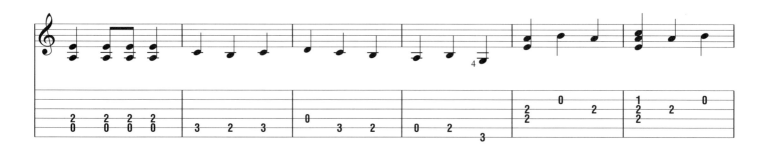

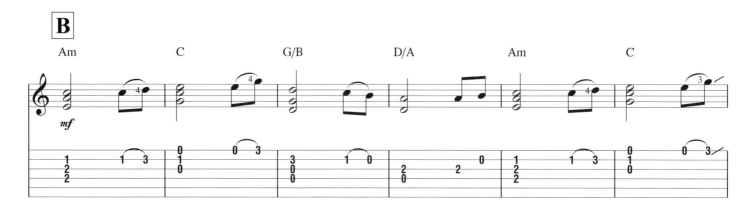

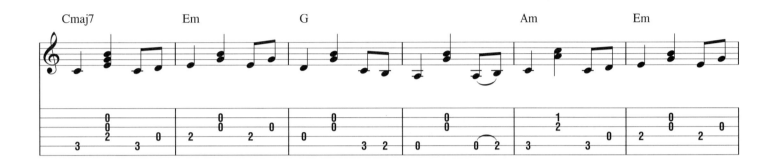

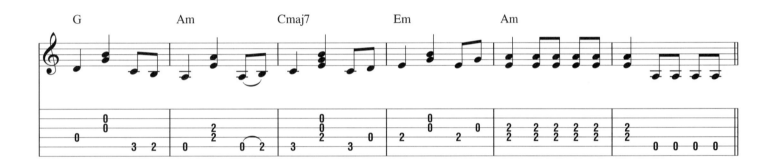

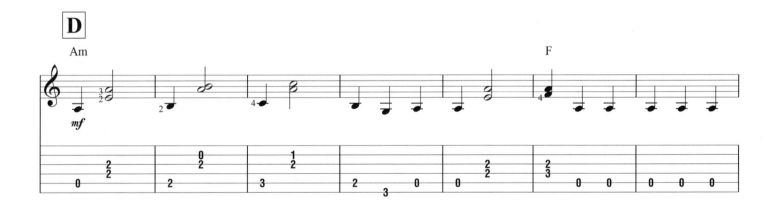

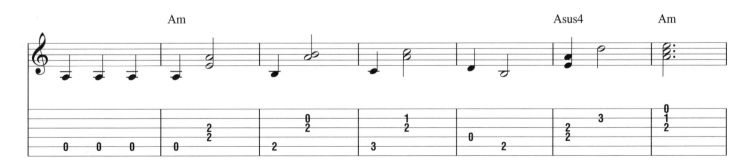

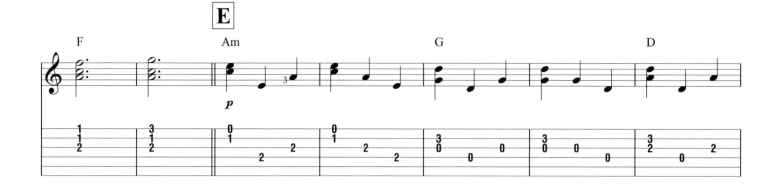

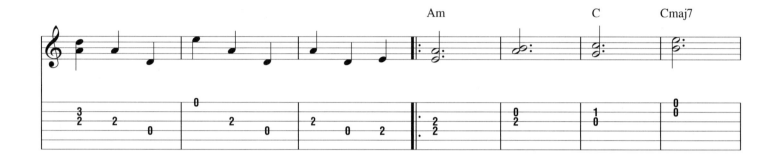

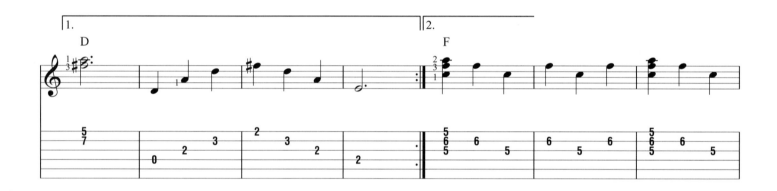

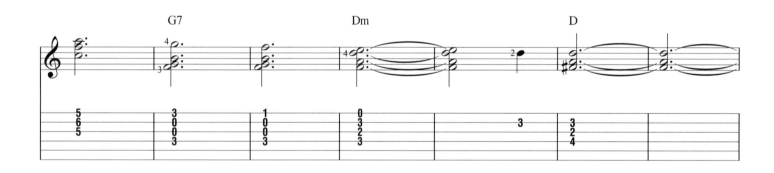

Theme from Fallout ® 4

Composed by Inon Zur

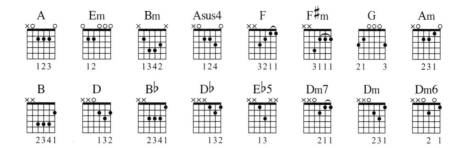

*Capo III

Strum Pattern: 1, 2
Pick Pattern: 2

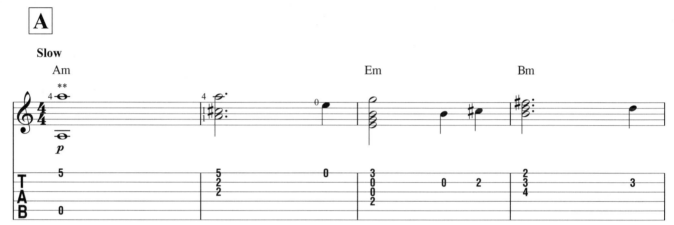

*Optional: To match recording, place capo at 3rd fret.
    **w/ pick & finger

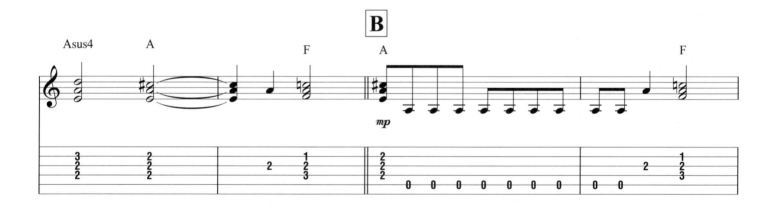

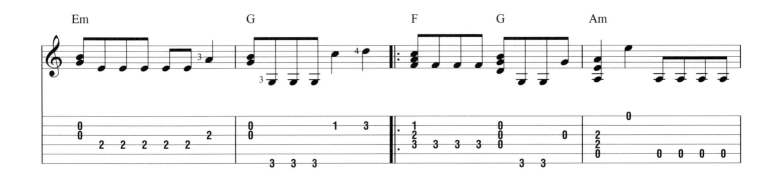

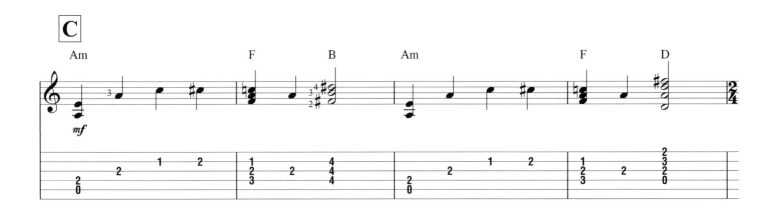

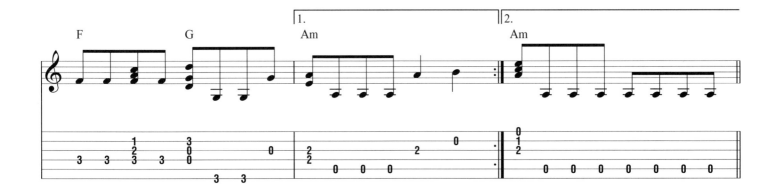

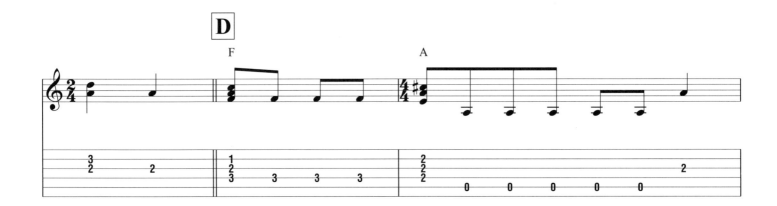

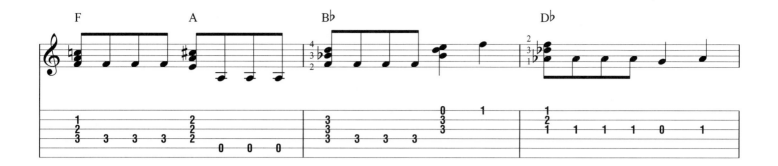

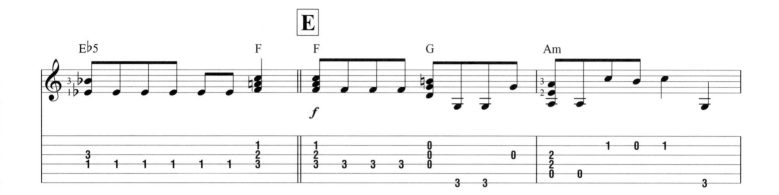

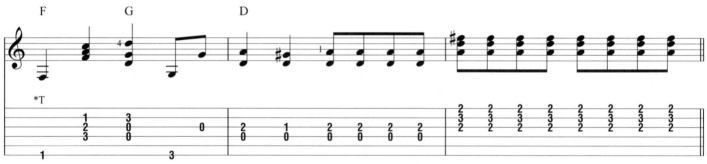

*Optional: T = Thumb on 6th string

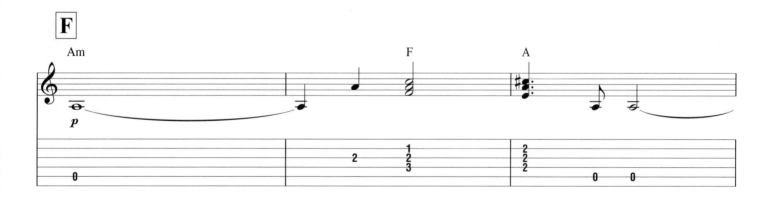

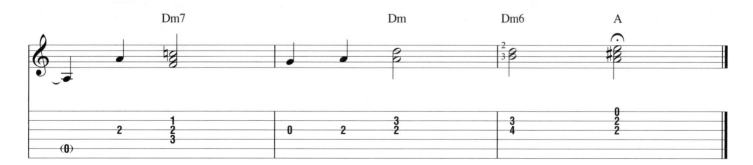

Eyes on Me
from FINAL FANTASY VIII

Music by Nobuo Uematsu
Lyrics by Kako Someya

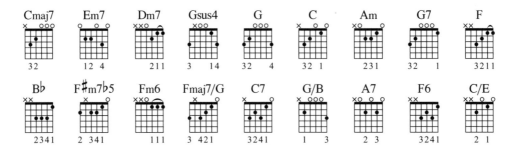

Strum Pattern: 6
Pick Pattern: 5

A

Moderately slow

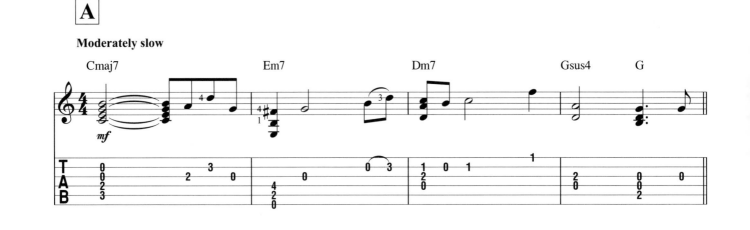

B

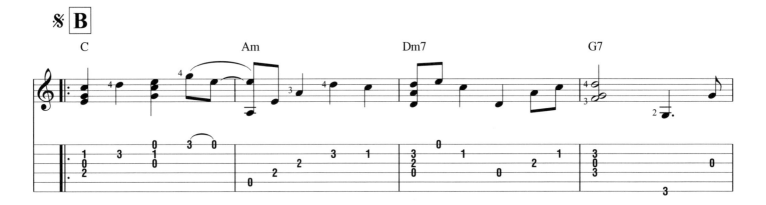

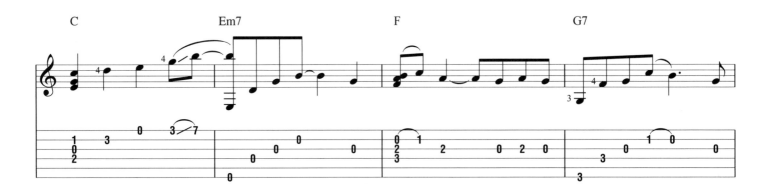

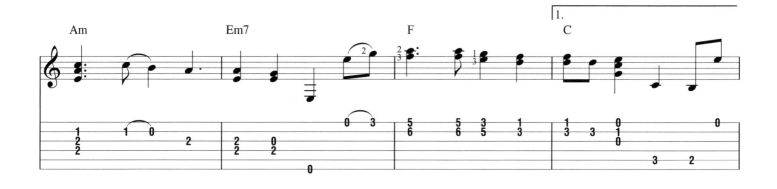

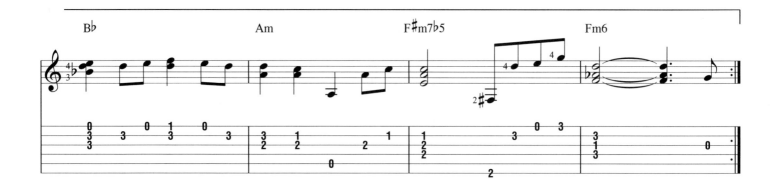

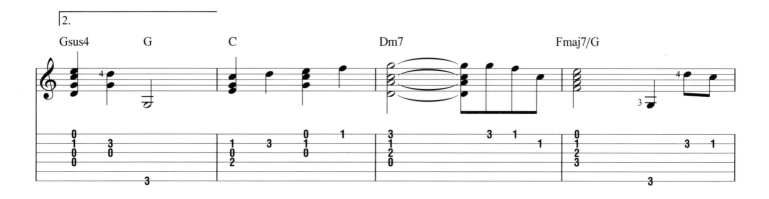

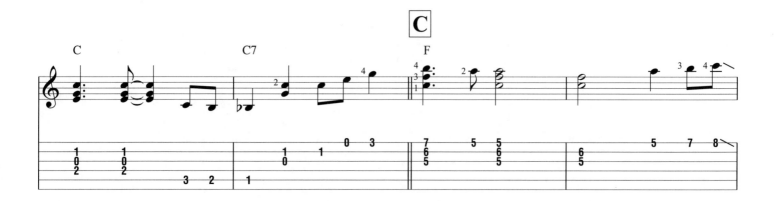

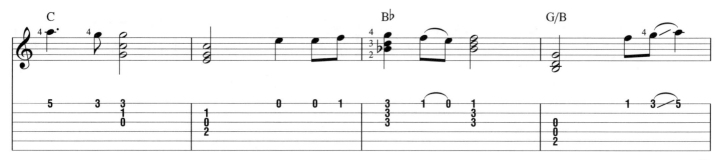

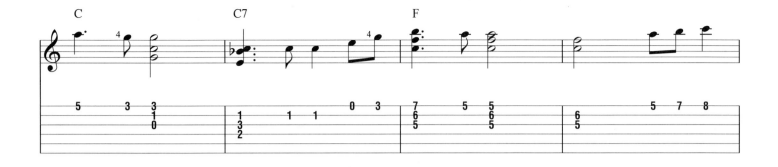

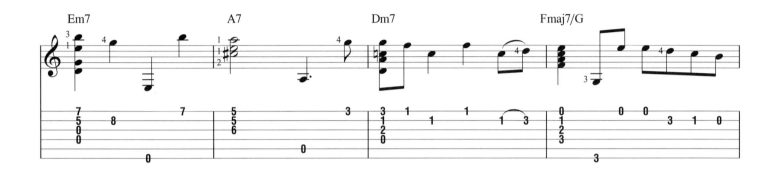

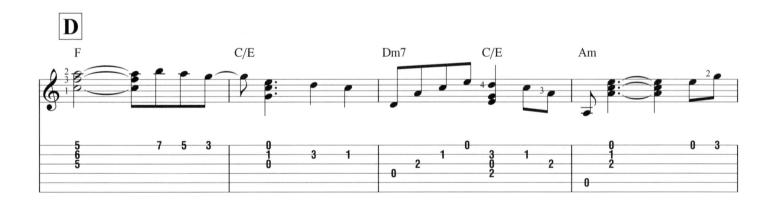

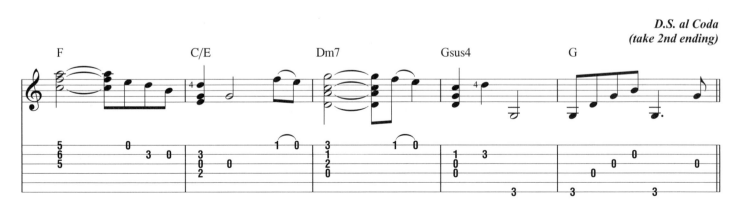

E

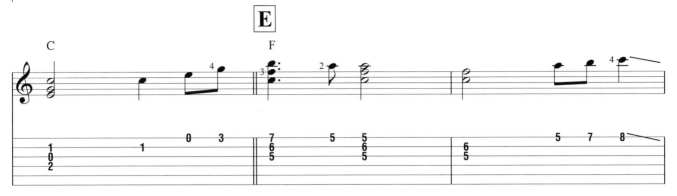

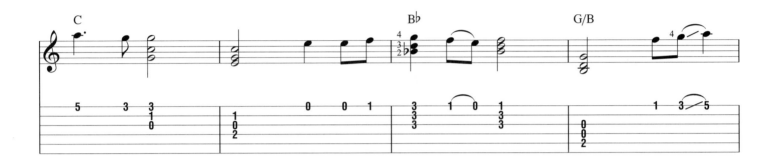

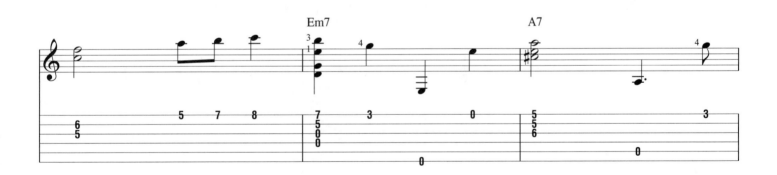

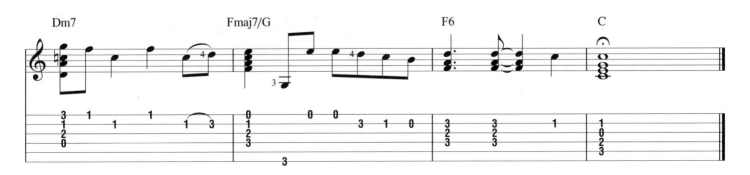

Main Theme (Final Fantasy I)
from FINAL FANTASY I

By Nobuo Uematsu

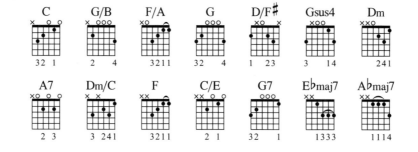

*Capo V

Strum Pattern: 3
Pick Pattern: 5

 A

Moderately

*Optional: To match recording, place capo at 5th fret.

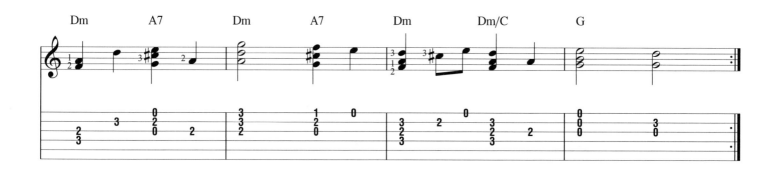

※ B

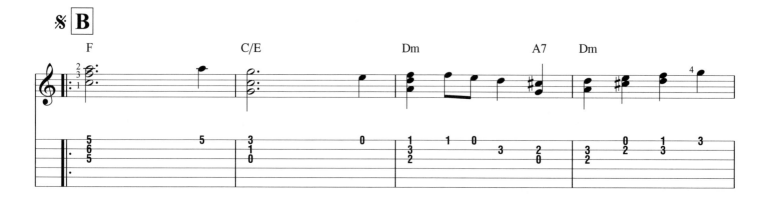

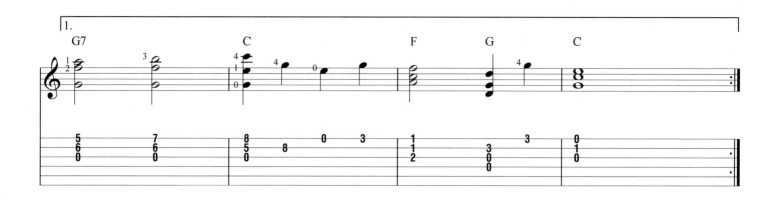

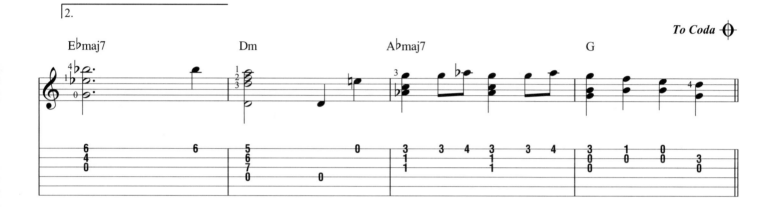

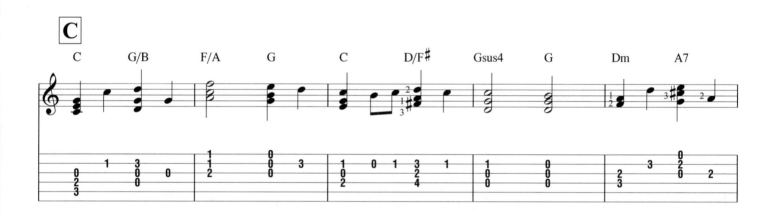

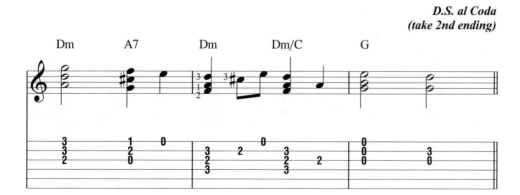

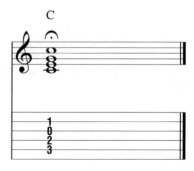

Main Theme (Final Fantasy VII)
from FINAL FANTASY VII

By Nobuo Uematsu

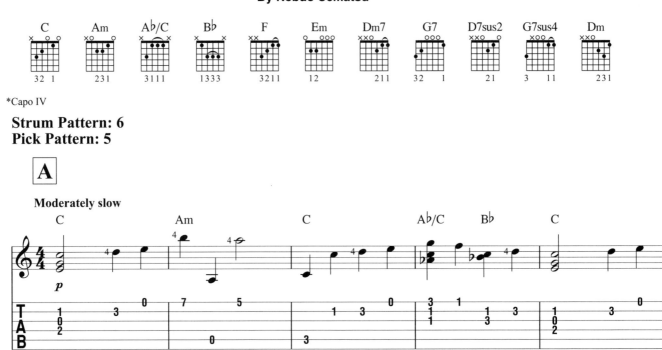

*Capo IV

Strum Pattern: 6
Pick Pattern: 5

A

Moderately slow

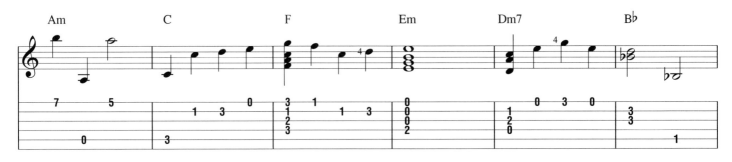

*Optional: To match recording, place capo at 4th fret.

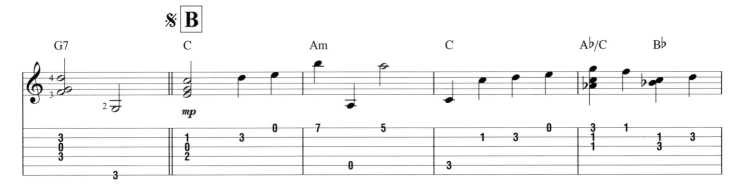

B

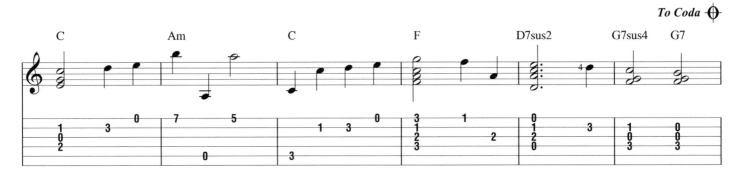

To Coda

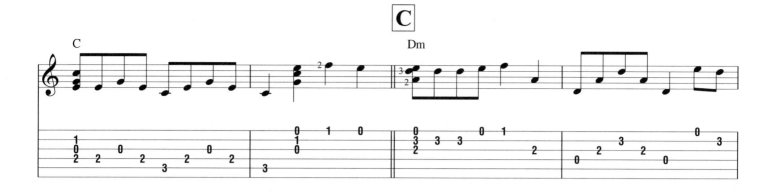

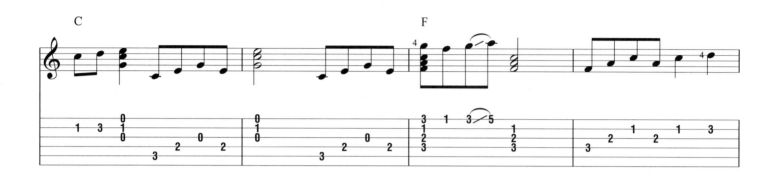

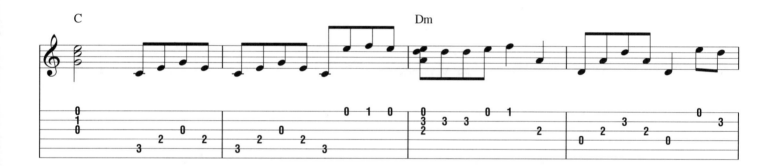

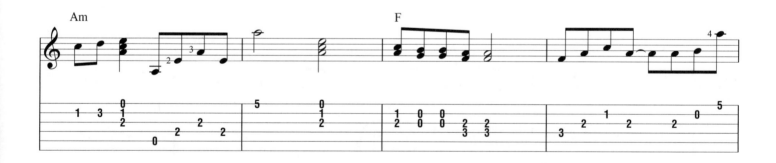

D.S. al Coda

⊕ **Coda**

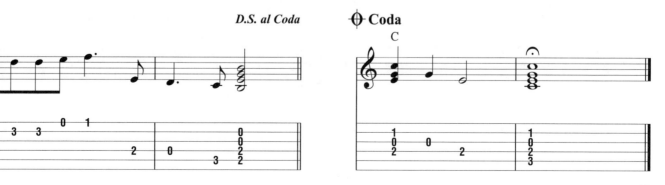

Megalovania
from UNDERTALE ®

Music by Toby Fox

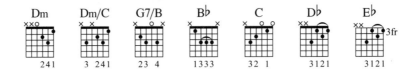

Strum Pattern: 5
Pick Pattern: 1

A

Moderately

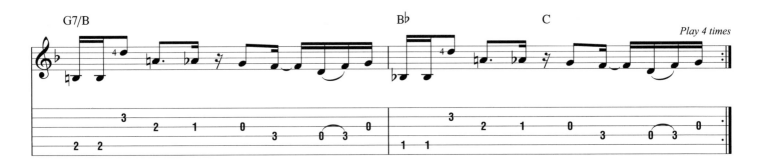

B

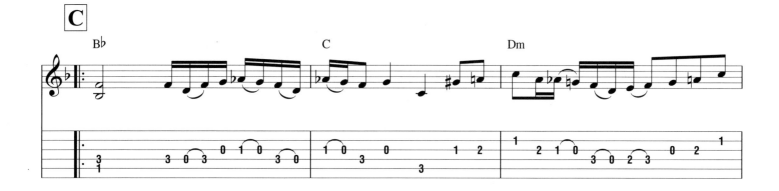

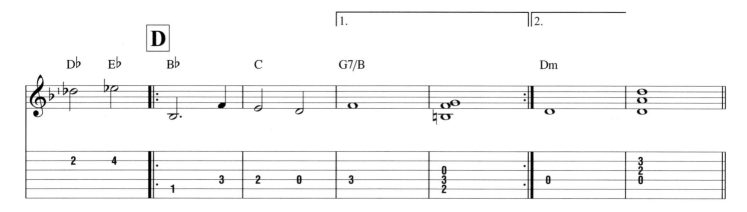

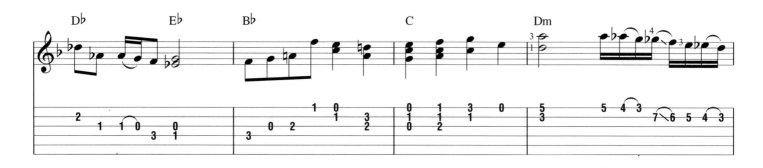

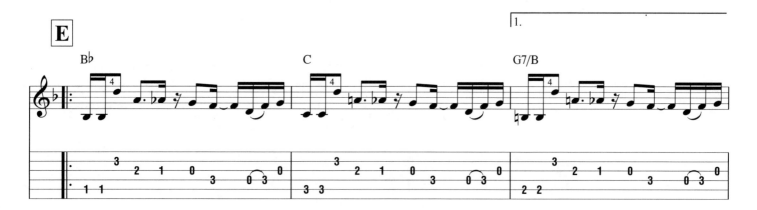

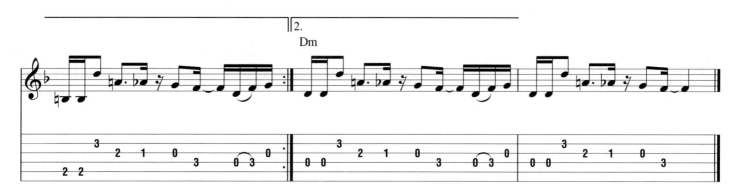

Sadness and Sorrow
from the television series NARUTO

By Purojekuto Musashi

Strum Pattern: 2, 5
Pick Pattern: 2, 5

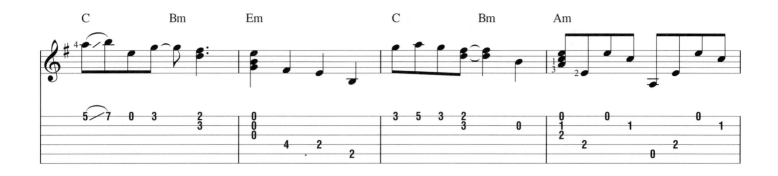

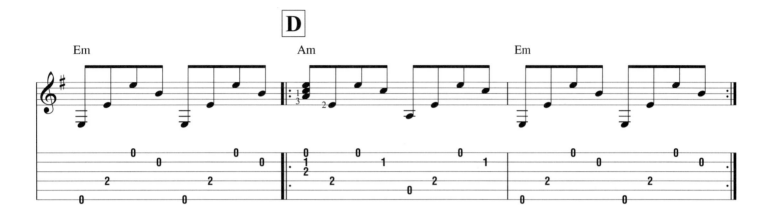

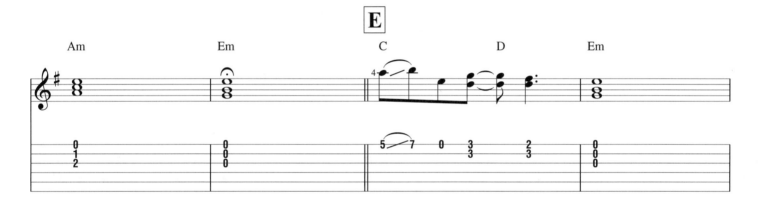

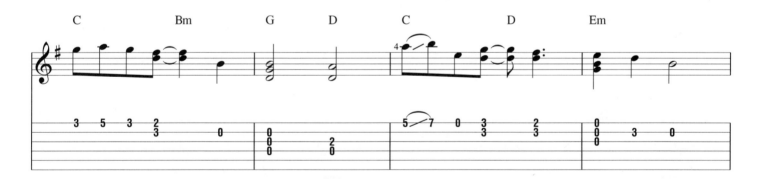

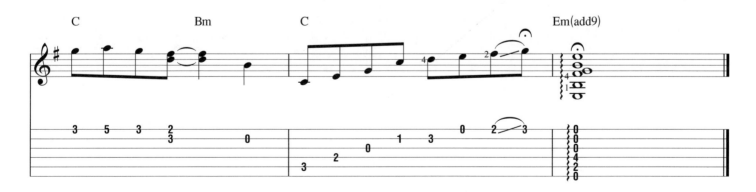

Splinter Cell: Conviction

Words and Music by Kaveh Cohen and Michael Nielsen

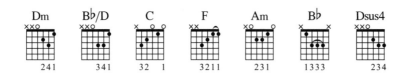

Strum Pattern: 5, 6
Pick Pattern: 4

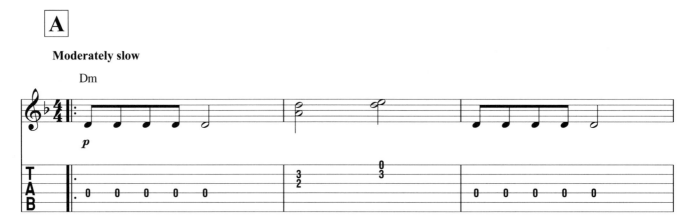

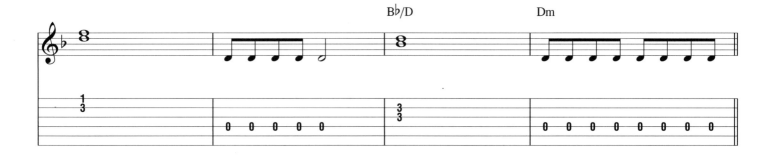

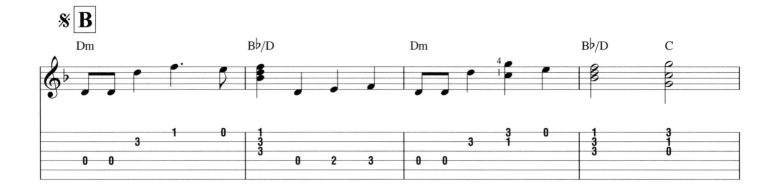

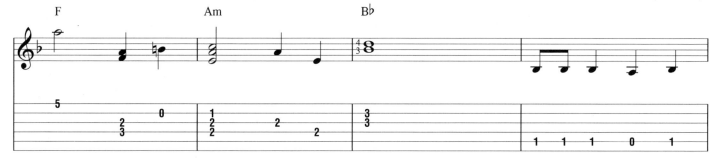

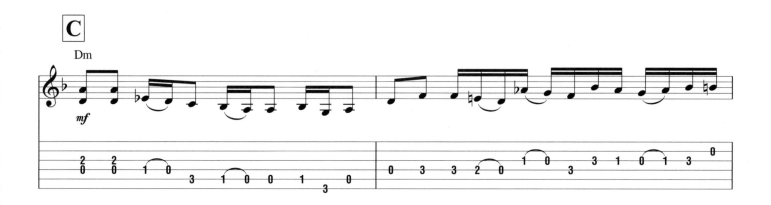

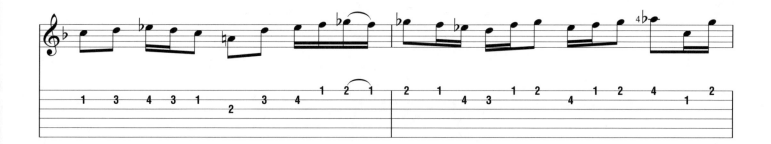

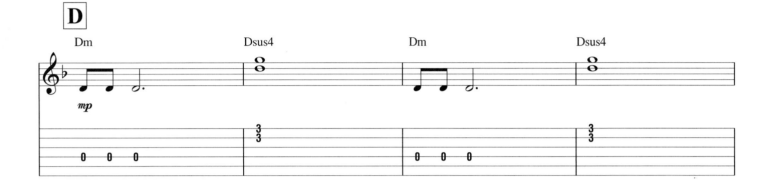

D

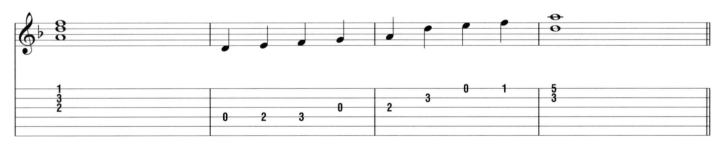

D.S. al Coda

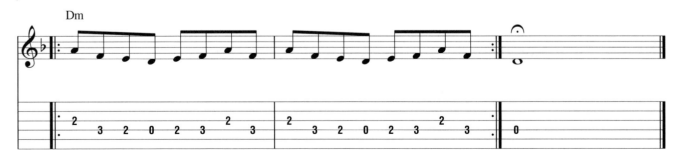

56

That's the Way It Is

from RED DEAD REDEMPTION II

Words and Music by Daniel Lanois and Rocco DeLuca

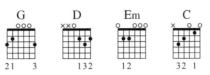

Strum Pattern: 6
Pick Pattern: 5

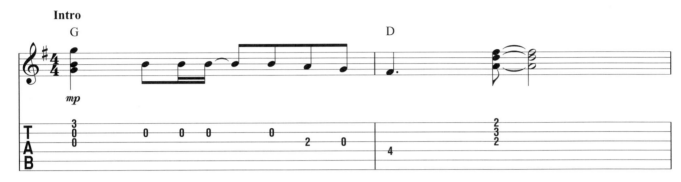

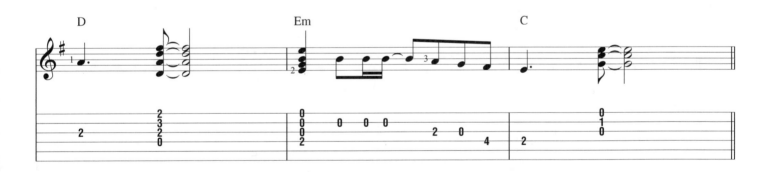

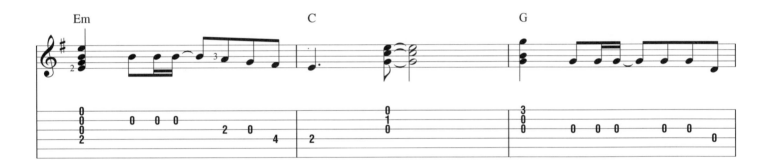

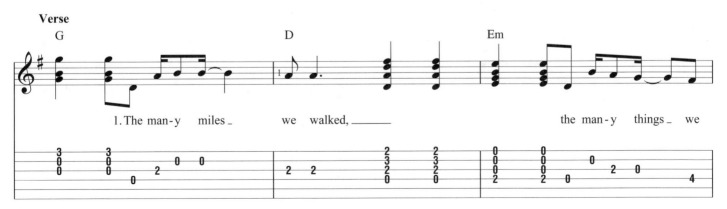

1. The man-y miles ___ we walked, ___ the man-y things ___ we

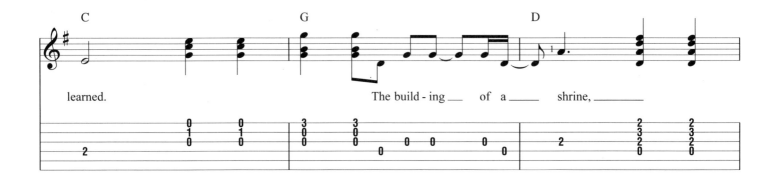

learned.   The build-ing __ of a __ shrine, __

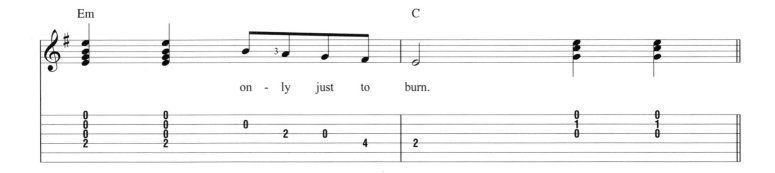

on - ly   just   to   burn.

Chorus

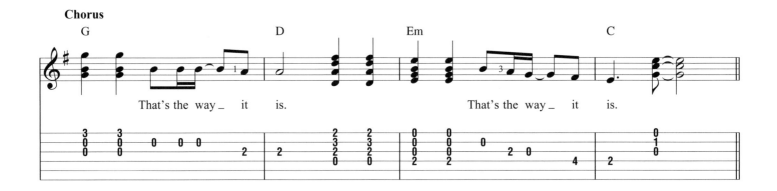

That's the way _ it   is.   That's the way _ it   is.

Interlude

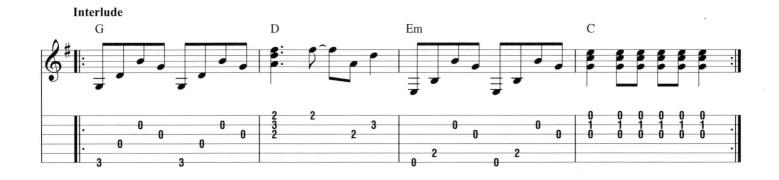

Verse

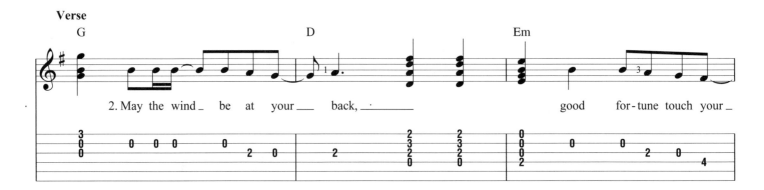

2. May the wind _ be   at   your __ back, __   good   for - tune touch your _

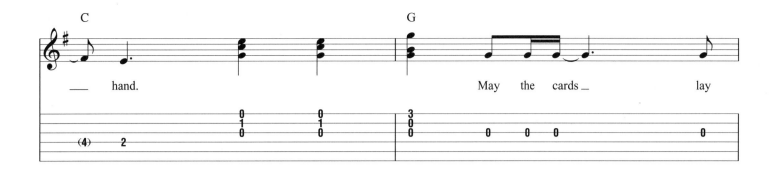

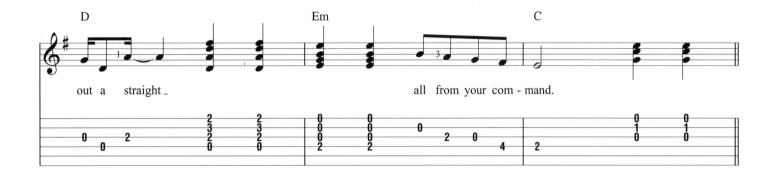

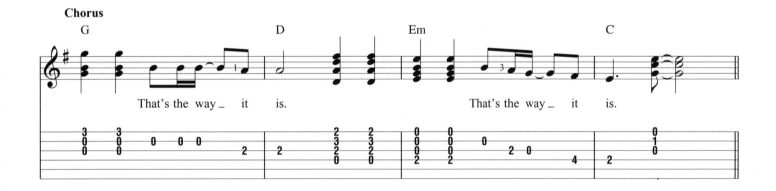

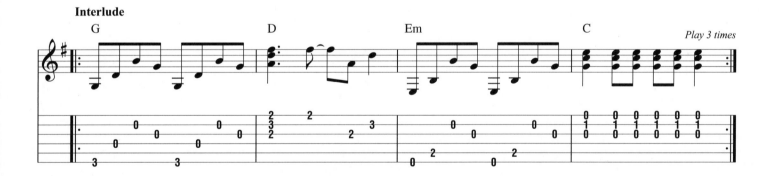

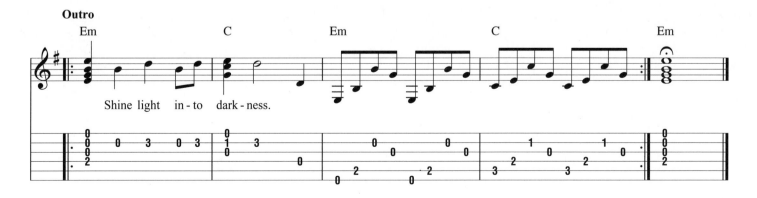

EASY GUITAR WITH NOTES & TAB

This series features simplified arrangements with notes, tab, chord charts, and strum and pick patterns.

MIXED FOLIOS

00702287	Acoustic	$16.99
00702002	Acoustic Rock Hits for Easy Guitar	$15.99
00702166	All-Time Best Guitar Collection	$19.99
00702232	Best Acoustic Songs for Easy Guitar	$14.99
00119835	Best Children's Songs	$16.99
00702233	Best Hard Rock Songs	$15.99
00703055	The Big Book of Nursery Rhymes & Children's Songs	$16.99
00322179	The Big Easy Book of Classic Rock Guitar	$24.95
00698978	Big Christmas Collection	$17.99
00702394	Bluegrass Songs for Easy Guitar	$12.99
00289632	Bohemian Rhapsody	$17.99
00703387	Celtic Classics	$14.99
00224808	Chart Hits of 2016-2017	$14.99
00267383	Chart Hits of 2017-2018	$14.99
00702149	Children's Christian Songbook	$9.99
00702028	Christmas Classics	$8.99
00101779	Christmas Guitar	$14.99
00702185	Christmas Hits	$10.99
00702141	Classic Rock	$8.95
00159642	Classical Melodies	$12.99
00253933	Disney/Pixar's Coco	$16.99
00702203	CMT's 100 Greatest Country Songs	$29.99

00702283	The Contemporary Christian Collection	$16.99
00196954	Contemporary Disney	$16.99
00702239	Country Classics for Easy Guitar	$22.99
00702257	Easy Acoustic Guitar Songs	$14.99
00702280	Easy Guitar Tab White Pages	$29.99
00702041	Favorite Hymns for Easy Guitar	$10.99
00222701	Folk Pop Songs	$14.99
00140841	4-Chord Hymns for Guitar	$9.99
00702281	4 Chord Rock	$10.99
00126894	Frozen	$14.99
00702286	Glee	$16.99
00699374	Gospel Favorites	$16.99
00702160	The Great American Country Songbook	$16.99
00702050	Great Classical Themes for Easy Guitar	$8.99
00702116	Greatest Hymns for Guitar	$10.99
00275088	The Greatest Showman	$17.99
00148030	Halloween Guitar Songs	$14.99
00702273	Irish Songs	$12.99
00192503	Jazz Classics for Easy Guitar	$14.99
00702275	Jazz Favorites for Easy Guitar	$15.99
00702274	Jazz Standards for Easy Guitar	$16.99
00702162	Jumbo Easy Guitar Songbook	$19.99
00232285	La La Land	$16.99
00702258	Legends of Rock	$14.99
00702189	MTV's 100 Greatest Pop Songs	$24.95

00702272	1950s Rock	$15.99
00702271	1960s Rock	$15.99
00702270	1970s Rock	$16.99
00702269	1980s Rock	$15.99
00702268	1990s Rock	$19.99
00109725	Once	$14.99
00702187	Selections from O Brother Where Art Thou?	$17.99
00702178	100 Songs for Kids	$14.99
00702515	Pirates of the Caribbean	$14.99
00702125	Praise and Worship for Guitar	$10.99
00287930	Songs from *A Star Is Born, The Greatest Showman, La La Land,* and More Movie Musicals	$16.99
00702285	Southern Rock Hits	$12.99
00156420	Star Wars Music	$14.99
00121535	30 Easy Celtic Guitar Solos	$15.99
00702220	Today's Country Hits	$12.99
00121900	Today's Women of Pop & Rock	$14.99
00244654	Top Hits of 2017	$14.99
00283786	Top Hits of 2018	$14.99
00702294	Top Worship Hits	$15.99
00702255	VH1's 100 Greatest Hard Rock Songs	$27.99
00702175	VH1's 100 Greatest Songs of Rock and Roll	$24.99
00702253	Wicked	$12.99

ARTIST COLLECTIONS

00702267	AC/DC for Easy Guitar	$15.99
00702598	Adele for Easy Guitar	$15.99
00156221	Adele – 25	$16.99
00702040	Best of the Allman Brothers	$16.99
00702865	J.S. Bach for Easy Guitar	$14.99
00702169	Best of The Beach Boys	$12.99
00702292	The Beatles — 1	$19.99
00125796	Best of Chuck Berry	$15.99
00702201	The Essential Black Sabbath	$12.95
02501615	Zac Brown Band — The Foundation	$16.99
02501621	Zac Brown Band — You Get What You Give	$16.99
00702043	Best of Johnny Cash	$16.99
00702090	Eric Clapton's Best	$12.99
00702086	Eric Clapton — from the Album Unplugged	$15.99
00702202	The Essential Eric Clapton	$14.99
00702250	blink-182 — Greatest Hits	$15.99
00702053	Best of Patsy Cline	$15.99
00222697	Very Best of Coldplay – 2nd Edition	$14.99
00702229	The Very Best of Creedence Clearwater Revival	$15.99
00702145	Best of Jim Croce	$15.99
00702278	Crosby, Stills & Nash	$12.99
14042809	Bob Dylan	$14.99
00702276	Fleetwood Mac — Easy Guitar Collection	$14.99
00139462	The Very Best of Grateful Dead	$15.99
00702136	Best of Merle Haggard	$14.99
00702227	Jimi Hendrix — Smash Hits	$16.99
00702288	Best of Hillsong United	$12.99
00702236	Best of Antonio Carlos Jobim	$14.99
00702245	Elton John — Greatest Hits 1970-2002	$17.99

00129855	Jack Johnson	$16.99
00702204	Robert Johnson	$10.99
00702234	Selections from Toby Keith — 35 Biggest Hits	$12.95
00702003	Kiss	$12.99
00702216	Lynyrd Skynyrd	$15.99
00702182	The Essential Bob Marley	$14.99
00146081	Maroon 5	$14.99
00121925	Bruno Mars — Unorthodox Jukebox	$12.99
00702248	Paul McCartney — All the Best	$14.99
00702129	Songs of Sarah McLachlan	$12.95
00125484	The Best of MercyMe	$12.99
02501316	Metallica — Death Magnetic	$19.99
00702209	Steve Miller Band — Young Hearts (Greatest Hits)	$12.95
00124167	Jason Mraz	$15.99
00702096	Best of Nirvana	$15.99
00702211	The Offspring — Greatest Hits	$12.95
00138026	One Direction	$14.99
00702030	Best of Roy Orbison	$15.99
00702144	Best of Ozzy Osbourne	$14.99
00702279	Tom Petty	$12.99
00102911	Pink Floyd	$16.99
00702139	Elvis Country Favorites	$16.99
00702293	The Very Best of Prince	$15.99
00699415	Best of Queen for Guitar	$15.99
00109279	Best of R.E.M.	$14.99
00702208	Red Hot Chili Peppers — Greatest Hits	$15.99
00198960	The Rolling Stones	$16.99
00174793	The Very Best of Santana	$14.99
00702196	Best of Bob Seger	$12.95
00146046	Ed Sheeran	$14.99
00702252	Frank Sinatra — Nothing But the Best	$12.99

00702010	Best of Rod Stewart	$16.99
00702049	Best of George Strait	$14.99
00702259	Taylor Swift for Easy Guitar	$15.99
00254499	Taylor Swift – Easy Guitar Anthology	$19.99
00702260	Taylor Swift — Fearless	$14.99
00139727	Taylor Swift — 1989	$17.99
00115960	Taylor Swift — Red	$16.99
00253667	Taylor Swift — Reputation	$17.99
00702290	Taylor Swift — Speak Now	$16.99
00232849	Chris Tomlin Collection – 2nd Edition	$14.99
00702226	Chris Tomlin — See the Morning	$12.95
00148643	Train	$14.99
00702427	U2 — 18 Singles	$16.99
00702108	Best of Stevie Ray Vaughan	$16.99
00279005	The Who	$14.99
00702123	Best of Hank Williams	$14.99
00194548	Best of John Williams	$14.99
00702111	Stevie Wonder — Guitar Collection	$9.95
00702228	Neil Young — Greatest Hits	$15.99
00119133	Neil Young — Harvest	$14.99

Prices, contents and availability subject to change without notice.

HAL•LEONARD®

Visit Hal Leonard online at **halleonard.com**

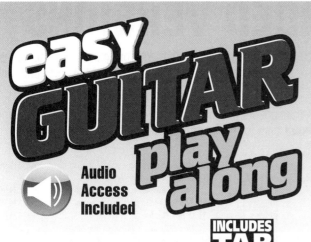

easy GUITAR play along

Audio Access Included

The *Easy Guitar Play Along*® series features streamlined transcriptions of your favorite songs. Just follow the tab, listen to the audio to hear how the guitar should sound, and then play along using the backing tracks. Playback tools are provided for slowing down the tempo without changing pitch and looping challenging parts. The melody and lyrics are included in the book so that you can sing or simply follow along.

INCLUDES TAB

1. ROCK CLASSICS

Jailbreak • Living After Midnight • Mississippi Queen • Rocks Off • Runnin' Down a Dream • Smoke on the Water • Strutter • Up Around the Bend.
00702560 Book/CD Pack....... $14.99

2. ACOUSTIC TOP HITS

About a Girl • I'm Yours • The Lazy Song • The Scientist • 21 Guns • Upside Down • What I Got • Wonderwall.
00702569 Book/CD Pack....... $14.99

3. ROCK HITS

All the Small Things • Best of You • Brain Stew (The Godzilla Remix) • Californication • Island in the Sun • Plush • Smells Like Teen Spirit • Use Somebody.
00702570 Book/CD Pack....... $14.99

4. ROCK 'N' ROLL

Blue Suede Shoes • I Get Around • I'm a Believer • Jailhouse Rock • Oh, Pretty Woman • Peggy Sue • Runaway • Wake Up Little Susie.
00702572 Book/CD Pack....... $14.99

6. CHRISTMAS SONGS

Have Yourself a Merry Little Christmas • A Holly Jolly Christmas • The Little Drummer Boy • Run Rudolph Run • Santa Claus Is Comin' to Town • Silver and Gold • Sleigh Ride • Winter Wonderland.
00101879 Book/CD Pack......... $14.99

7. BLUES SONGS FOR BEGINNERS

Come On (Part 1) • Double Trouble • Gangster of Love • I'm Ready • Let Me Love You Baby • Mary Had a Little Lamb • San-Ho-Zay • T-Bone Shuffle.
00103235 Book/Online Audio $14.99

8. ACOUSTIC SONGS FOR BEGINNERS

Barely Breathing • Drive • Everlong • Good Riddance (Time of Your Life) • Hallelujah • Hey There Delilah • Lake of Fire • Photograph.
00103240 Book/CD Pack $15.99

9. ROCK SONGS FOR BEGINNERS

Are You Gonna Be My Girl • Buddy Holly • Everybody Hurts • In Bloom • Otherside • The Rock Show • Santa Monica • When I Come Around.
00103255 Book/CD Pack.....$14.99

10. GREEN DAY

Basket Case • Boulevard of Broken Dreams • Good Riddance (Time of Your Life) • Holiday • Longview • 21 Guns • Wake Me up When September Ends • When I Come Around.
00122322 Book/CD Pack $14.99

11. NIRVANA

All Apologies • Come As You Are • Heart Shaped Box • Lake of Fire • Lithium • The Man Who Sold the World • Rape Me • Smells Like Teen Spirit.
00122325 Book/Online Audio $14.99

13. AC/DC

Back in Black • Dirty Deeds Done Dirt Cheap • For Those About to Rock (We Salute You) • Hells Bells • Highway to Hell • Rock and Roll Ain't Noise Pollution • T.N.T. • You Shook Me All Night Long.
14042895 Book/Online Audio........$16.99

14. JIMI HENDRIX – SMASH HITS

All Along the Watchtower • Can You See Me • Crosstown Traffic • Fire • Foxey Lady • Hey Joe • Manic Depression • Purple Haze • Red House • Remember • Stone Free • The Wind Cries Mary.
00130591 Book/Online Audio........$24.99

HAL•LEONARD®

www.halleonard.com

GUITAR RECORDED VERSIONS®

Guitar Recorded Versions® are note-for-note transcriptions of guitar music taken directly off recordings. This series, one of the most popular in print today, features some of the greatest guitar players and groups from blues and rock to country and jazz.

Guitar Recorded Versions are transcribed by the best transcribers in the business. Every book contains notes and tablature unless otherwise marked. Visit **www.halleonard.com** for our complete selection.

00690684	Jethro Tull – Aqualung	$19.99
00690693	Jethro Tull Guitar Anthology	$22.99
00691182	Jethro Tull – Stand Up	$22.99
00690898	John 5 – The Devil Knows My Name	$22.95
00690814	John 5 – Songs for Sanity	$19.95
00690751	John 5 – Vertigo	$19.95
00694912	Eric Johnson – Ah Via Musicom	$24.99
00690660	Best of Eric Johnson	$22.99
00691076	Eric Johnson – Up Close	$22.99
00690169	Eric Johnson – Venus Isle	$22.95
00122439	Jack Johnson – From Here to Now to You	$22.99
00690846	Jack Johnson and Friends – Sing-A-Longs and Lullabies for the Film Curious George	$19.95
00690271	Robert Johnson – The New Transcriptions	$24.99
00699131	Best of Janis Joplin	$19.95
00690427	Best of Judas Priest	$24.99
00690277	Best of Kansas	$19.99
00690911	Best of Phil Keaggy	$24.99
00690727	Toby Keith Guitar Collection	$19.99
00120814	Killswitch Engage – Disarm the Descent	$22.99
00690504	Very Best of Albert King	$19.95
00124869	Albert King with Stevie Ray Vaughan – In Session	$22.99
00130447	B.B. King – Live at the Regal	$17.99
00690444	B.B. King & Eric Clapton – Riding with the King	$24.99
00690134	Freddie King Collection	$19.99
00691062	Kings of Leon – Come Around Sundown	$22.99
00690157	Kiss – Alive!	$19.95
00690356	Kiss – Alive II	$22.99
00694903	Best of Kiss for Guitar	$24.99
00690355	Kiss – Destroyer	$16.95
00291163	The Very Best of Kiss	$22.99
00690164	Mark Knopfler Guitar – Vol. 1	$24.99
00690163	Mark Knopfler/Chet Atkins – Neck and Neck	$24.99
00690780	Korn – Greatest Hits, Volume 1	$24.99
00690377	Kris Kristofferson Collection	$19.99
00690834	Lamb of God – Ashes of the Wake	$22.99
00690875	Lamb of God – Sacrament	$22.99
00690977	Ray LaMontagne – Gossip in the Grain	$19.99
00691057	Ray LaMontagne and the Pariah Dogs – God Willin' & The Creek Don't Rise	$22.99
00690922	Linkin Park – Minutes to Midnight	$19.99
00114563	The Lumineers	$22.99
00690525	Best of George Lynch	$24.99
00690955	Lynyrd Skynyrd – All-Time Greatest Hits	$24.99
00694954	New Best of Lynyrd Skynyrd	$22.99
00690577	Yngwie Malmsteen – Anthology	$27.99
00209846	Mammoth Metal Guitar Tab Anthology	$29.99
00690754	Marilyn Manson – Lest We Forget	$19.99
00694956	Bob Marley – Legend	$19.95
00694945	Bob Marley – Songs of Freedom	$24.95
00690657	Maroon 5 – Songs About Jane	$19.95
00690989	Mastodon – Crack the Skye	$24.99
00236690	Mastodon – Emperor of Sand	$22.99
00119220	Brent Mason – Hot Wired	$19.99
00236690	Mastodon – Emperor of Sand	$22.99
00691176	Mastodon – The Hunter	$22.99
00137718	Mastodon – Once More 'Round the Sun	$22.99
00691942	Andy McKee – Art of Motion	$24.99
00691034	Andy McKee – Joyland	$19.99
00120080	The Don McLean Songbook	$19.99
00694952	Megadeth – Countdown to Extinction	$24.99
00690244	Megadeth – Cryptic Writings	$19.95
00276065	Megadeth – Greatest Hits: Back to the Start	$24.99
00694951	Megadeth – Rust in Peace	$24.99
00690011	Megadeth – Youthanasia	$22.99
00690505	John Mellencamp Guitar Collection	$19.99
00209876	Metallica – Hardwired... To Self-Destruct	$22.99
00690562	Pat Metheny – Bright Size Life	$19.95
00691073	Pat Metheny with Christian McBride & Antonion Sanchez – Day Trip/Tokyo Day Trip Live	$22.99
00690646	Pat Metheny – One Quiet Night	$19.95
00690559	Pat Metheny – Question & Answer	$22.99
00118836	Pat Metheny – Unity Band	$22.99
00102590	Pat Metheny – What's It All About	$22.99
00690040	Steve Miller Band Greatest Hits	$19.99
00119338	Ministry Guitar Tab Collection	$24.99
00102591	Wes Montgomery Guitar Anthology	$24.99
00694802	Gary Moore – Still Got the Blues	$24.99
00691005	Best of Motion City Soundtrack	$19.99
00129884	Jason Mraz – Yes!	$22.99
00691070	Mumford & Sons – Sigh No More	$22.99
00118196	Muse – The 2nd Law	$19.99
00690996	My Morning Jacket Collection	$19.99
00690984	Matt Nathanson – Some Mad Hope	$22.99
00690611	Nirvana	$22.95
00694895	Nirvana – Bleach	$19.99
00694913	Nirvana – In Utero	$19.99
00694883	Nirvana – Nevermind	$19.99
00690026	Nirvana – Unplugged in New York	$19.99
00265439	Nothing More – Guitar & Bass Tab Collection	$24.99
00307163	Oasis – Time Flies... 1994-2009	$24.99
00243349	The Best of Opeth	$22.99
00691052	Roy Orbison – Black & White Night	$22.99
00694847	Best of Ozzy Osbourne	$24.99
00690933	Best of Brad Paisley	$24.99
00690995	Brad Paisley – Play: The Guitar Album	$24.99
00690939	Christopher Parkening – Solo Pieces	$19.99
00690594	Best of Les Paul	$22.99
00694855	Pearl Jam – Ten	$22.99
00690439	A Perfect Circle – Mer De Noms	$19.99
00690725	Best of Carl Perkins	$19.99
00690499	Tom Petty – Definitive Guitar Collection	$19.99
00690176	Phish – Billy Breathes	$24.99
00121933	Pink Floyd – Acoustic Guitar Collection	$24.99
00690428	Pink Floyd – Dark Side of the Moon	$19.95
00244637	Pink Floyd – Guitar Anthology	$22.99
00239799	Pink Floyd – The Wall	$24.99
00690789	Best of Poison	$19.99
00690299	Best of Elvis: The King of Rock 'n' Roll	$19.99
00692535	Elvis Presley	$19.95
00690925	The Very Best of Prince	$22.99
00690003	Classic Queen	$24.95
00694975	Queen – Greatest Hits	$25.99
00254332	Queens of the Stone Age – Villains	$22.99
00690670	Very Best of Queensryche	$24.99
00690878	The Raconteurs – Broken Boy Soldiers	$19.95
00109303	Radiohead Guitar Anthology	$24.99
00694910	Rage Against the Machine	$22.99
00119834	Rage Against the Machine – Guitar Anthology	$22.99
00690179	Rancid – And Out Come the Wolves	$24.99
00690426	Best of Ratt	$19.95
00690055	Red Hot Chili Peppers – Blood Sugar Sex Magik	$19.99
00690584	Red Hot Chili Peppers – By the Way	$22.99
00690379	Red Hot Chili Peppers – Californication	$19.99
00690673	Red Hot Chili Peppers – Greatest Hits	$22.99
00690090	Red Hot Chili Peppers – One Hot Minute	$22.95
00691166	Red Hot Chili Peppers – I'm with You	$22.99
00690852	Red Hot Chili Peppers – Stadium Arcadium	$27.99
00690511	Django Reinhardt – The Definitive Collection	$22.99
00690643	Relient K – Two Lefts Don't Make a Right ... But Three Do	$19.95
00690260	Jimmie Rodgers Guitar Collection	$22.99
14041901	Rodrigo Y Gabriela and C.U.B.A. – Area 52	$24.99
00690014	Rolling Stones – Exile on Main Street	$24.99
00690631	Rolling Stones – Guitar Anthology	$29.99
00690685	David Lee Roth – Eat 'Em and Smile	$22.99
00174797	Santana – IV*	$22.99
00173534	Santana Guitar Anthology	$24.99
00690031	Santana's Greatest Hits	$19.95
00276350	Joe Satriani – What Happens Next	$24.99
00690796	Very Best of Michael Schenker	$19.95
00128870	Matt Schofield Guitar Tab Collection	$22.99
00690566	Best of Scorpions	$24.99
00690604	Bob Seger – Guitar Anthology	$22.99
00234543	Ed Sheeran – Divide	$19.99
00138870	Ed Sheeran – X	$19.99
00690803	Best of Kenny Wayne Shepherd Band	$22.99
00122218	Skillet – Rise	$22.99
00691114	Slash – Guitar Anthology	$27.99
00690872	Slayer – Christ Illusion	$19.95
00690813	Slayer – Guitar Collection	$19.99
00690419	Slipknot	$19.95
00690973	Slipknot – All Hope Is Gone	$22.99
00690330	Social Distortion – Live at the Roxy	$19.95
00120004	Best of Steely Dan	$24.99
00694921	Best of Steppenwolf	$22.95
00690655	Best of Mike Stern	$24.99
14041588	Cat Stevens – Tea for the Tillerman	$19.99
00690949	Rod Stewart Guitar Anthology	$19.99
00690520	Styx Guitar Collection	$19.95
00120081	Sublime	$19.99
00690992	Sublime – Robbin' the Hood	$19.99
00690519	SUM 41 – All Killer No Filler	$19.95
00691072	Best of Supertramp	$22.99
00142151	Taylor Swift – 1989	$22.99
00115957	Taylor Swift – Red	$21.99

RECORDED VERSIONS GUITAR®

AUTHENTIC TRANSCRIPTIONS WITH NOTES AND TABLATURE

00691063	Taylor Swift – Speak Now	$22.99
00690767	Switchfoot – The Beautiful Letdown	$19.95
00690531	System of a Down – Toxicity	$19.99
00694824	Best of James Taylor	$19.99
00694887	Best of Thin Lizzy	$19.99
00690891	30 Seconds to Mars – A Beautiful Lie	$19.95
00690233	The Merle Travis Collection	$22.99
00253237	Trivium – Guitar Tab Anthology	$24.99
00690683	Robin Trower – Bridge of Sighs	$19.99
00699191	U2 – Best of: 1980-1990	$19.99
00690732	U2 – Best of: 1990-2000	$19.95
00690894	U2 – 18 Singles	$22.99
00124461	Keith Urban – Guitar Anthology	$19.99
00690039	Steve Vai – Alien Love Secrets	$24.99
00690172	Steve Vai – Fire Garden	$24.95
00197570	Steve Vai – Modern Primitive	$29.99
00690881	Steve Vai – Real Illusions: Reflections	$27.99
00694904	Steve Vai – Sex and Religion	$24.95
00110385	Steve Vai – The Story of Light	$22.99
00690392	Steve Vai – The Ultra Zone	$19.95
00700555	Van Halen – Van Halen	$19.99
00690024	Stevie Ray Vaughan – Couldn't Stand the Weather	$19.99
00690116	Stevie Ray Vaughan – Guitar Collection	$24.95
00694879	Stevie Ray Vaughan – In the Beginning	$19.95
00660058	Stevie Ray Vaughan – Lightnin' Blues '83-'87	$27.99
00217455	Stevie Ray Vaughan – Plays Slow Blues	$19.99
00694835	Stevie Ray Vaughan – The Sky Is Crying	$22.95
00690025	Stevie Ray Vaughan – Soul to Soul	$19.95
00690015	Stevie Ray Vaughan – Texas Flood	$19.99
00109770	Volbeat Guitar Collection	$22.99
00121808	Volbeat – Outlaw Gentlemen & Shady Ladies	$22.99
00183213	Volbeat – Seal the Deal & Let's Boogie*	$19.99
00690132	The T-Bone Walker Collection	$19.99
00150209	Trans-Siberian Orchestra Guitar Anthology	$19.99
00694789	Muddy Waters – Deep Blues	$24.99
00152161	Doc Watson – Guitar Anthology	$22.99
00690071	Weezer (The Blue Album)	$19.99
00691046	Weezer – Rarities Edition	$22.99
00172118	Weezer (The White Album)*	$19.99
00117511	Whitesnake Guitar Collection	$24.99
00690447	Best of the Who	$24.99
00691941	The Who – Acoustic Guitar Collection	$22.99
00691006	Wilco Guitar Collection	$22.99
00691017	Wolfmother – Cosmic Egg	$22.99
00690319	Stevie Wonder – Hits	$22.99
00690596	Best of the Yardbirds	$19.99
00690916	The Best of Dwight Yoakam	$19.95
00691020	Neil Young – After the Goldrush	$22.99
00691019	Neil Young – Everybody Knows This Is Nowhere	$19.99
00690904	Neil Young – Harvest	$29.99
00691021	Neil Young – Harvest Moon	$22.99
00690905	Neil Young – Rust Never Sleeps	$19.99
00690443	Frank Zappa – Hot Rats	$19.99
00690624	Frank Zappa and the Mothers of Invention – One Size Fits All	$22.99
00690623	Frank Zappa – Over-Nite Sensation	$22.99
00121684	ZZ Top – Early Classics	$24.99
00690589	ZZ Top – Guitar Anthology	$24.99
00690960	ZZ Top Guitar Classics	$19.99

HAL•LEONARD®

*Tab transcriptions only.

Complete songlists and more at **www.halleonard.com**

Prices, contents, and availability subject to change without notice.

0719

HAL·LEONARD
GUITAR PLAY-ALONG

AUDIO ACCESS INCLUDED

This series will help you play your favorite songs quickly and easily. Just follow the tab and listen to the audio to the hear how the guitar should sound, and then play along using the separate backing tracks. Audio files also include software to slow down the tempo without changing pitch. The melody and lyrics are included in the book so that you can sing or simply follow along.

INCLUDES TAB

VOL. 1 – ROCK	00699570 / $16.99	
VOL. 2 – ACOUSTIC	00699569 / $16.99	
VOL. 3 – HARD ROCK	00699573 / $17.99	
VOL. 4 – POP/ROCK	00298615 / $16.99	
VOL. 6 – '90S ROCK	00699572 / $16.99	
VOL. 7 – BLUES	00699575 / $17.99	
VOL. 8 – ROCK	00699585 / $16.99	
VOL. 9 – EASY ACOUSTIC SONGS	00151708 / $16.99	
VOL. 10 – ACOUSTIC	00699586 / $16.95	
VOL. 13 – FOLK ROCK	00699581 / $16.99	
VOL. 14 – BLUES ROCK	00699582 / $16.99	
VOL. 15 – R&B	00699583 / $16.99	
VOL. 16 – JAZZ	00699584 / $15.95	
VOL. 17 – COUNTRY	00699588 / $16.99	
VOL. 18 – ACOUSTIC ROCK	00699577 / $15.95	
VOL. 20 – ROCKABILLY	00699580 / $16.99	
VOL. 21 – SANTANA	00174525 / $17.99	
VOL. 22 – CHRISTMAS	00699600 / $15.99	
VOL. 23 – SURF	00699635 / $15.99	
VOL. 24 – ERIC CLAPTON	00699649 / $17.99	
VOL. 25 – THE BEATLES	00198265 / $17.99	
VOL. 26 – ELVIS PRESLEY	00699643 / $16.99	
VOL. 27 – DAVID LEE ROTH	00699645 / $16.95	
VOL. 28 – GREG KOCH	00699646 / $17.99	
VOL. 29 – BOB SEGER	00699647 / $16.99	
VOL. 30 – KISS	00699644 / $16.99	
VOL. 32 – THE OFFSPRING	00699653 / $14.95	
VOL. 33 – ACOUSTIC CLASSICS	00699656 / $17.99	
VOL. 34 – CLASSIC ROCK	00699658 / $17.99	
VOL. 35 – HAIR METAL	00699660 / $17.99	
VOL. 36 – SOUTHERN ROCK	00699661 / $17.99	
VOL. 37 – ACOUSTIC UNPLUGGED	00699662 / $22.99	
VOL. 38 – BLUES	00699663 / $16.95	
VOL. 39 – '80S METAL	00699664 / $16.99	
VOL. 40 – INCUBUS	00699668 / $17.95	
VOL. 41 – ERIC CLAPTON	00699669 / $17.99	
VOL. 42 – COVER BAND HITS	00211597 / $16.99	
VOL. 43 – LYNYRD SKYNYRD	00699681 / $17.99	
VOL. 44 – JAZZ	00699689 / $16.99	
VOL. 45 – TV THEMES	00699718 / $14.95	
VOL. 46 – MAINSTREAM ROCK	00699722 / $16.95	
VOL. 47 – HENDRIX SMASH HITS	00699723 / $19.99	
VOL. 48 – AEROSMITH CLASSICS	00699724 / $17.99	
VOL. 49 – STEVIE RAY VAUGHAN	00699725 / $17.99	
VOL. 50 – VAN HALEN 1978-1984	00110269 / $17.99	
VOL. 51 – ALTERNATIVE '90S	00699727 / $14.99	
VOL. 52 – FUNK	00699728 / $15.99	
VOL. 53 – DISCO	00699729 / $14.99	
VOL. 54 – HEAVY METAL	00699730 / $16.99	
VOL. 55 – POP METAL	00699731 / $14.95	
VOL. 56 – FOO FIGHTERS	00699749 / $17.99	
VOL. 59 – CHET ATKINS	00702347 / $16.99	
VOL. 62 – CHRISTMAS CAROLS	00699798 / $12.95	
VOL. 63 – CREEDENCE CLEARWATER REVIVAL	00699802 / $16.99	
VOL. 64 – THE ULTIMATE OZZY OSBOURNE	00699803 / $17.99	
VOL. 66 – THE ROLLING STONES	00699807 / $17.99	
VOL. 67 – BLACK SABBATH	00699808 / $16.99	
VOL. 68 – PINK FLOYD – DARK SIDE OF THE MOON	00699809 / $16.99	
VOL. 73 – BLUESY ROCK	00699829 / $16.99	
VOL. 74 – SIMPLE STRUMMING SONGS	00151706 / $19.99	
VOL. 75 – TOM PETTY	00699882 / $16.99	

VOL. 76 – COUNTRY HITS	00699884 / $16.99
VOL. 77 – BLUEGRASS	00699910 / $15.99
VOL. 78 – NIRVANA	00700132 / $16.99
VOL. 79 – NEIL YOUNG	00700133 / $24.99
VOL. 80 – ACOUSTIC ANTHOLOGY	00700175 / $19.95
VOL. 81 – ROCK ANTHOLOGY	00700176 / $22.99
VOL. 82 – EASY SONGS	00700177 / $16.99
VOL. 84 – STEELY DAN	00700200 / $17.99
VOL. 85 – THE POLICE	00700269 / $16.99
VOL. 86 – BOSTON	00700465 / $16.99
VOL. 87 – ACOUSTIC WOMEN	00700763 / $14.99
VOL. 89 – REGGAE	00700468 / $15.99
VOL. 90 – CLASSICAL POP	00700469 / $14.99
VOL. 91 – BLUES INSTRUMENTALS	00700505 / $17.99
VOL. 92 – EARLY ROCK INSTRUMENTALS	00700506 / $15.99
VOL. 93 – ROCK INSTRUMENTALS	00700507 / $16.99
VOL. 94 – SLOW BLUES	00700508 / $16.99
VOL. 95 – BLUES CLASSICS	00700509 / $15.99
VOL. 96 – BEST COUNTRY HITS	00211615 / $16.99
VOL. 97 – CHRISTMAS CLASSICS	00236542 / $14.99
VOL. 99 – ZZ TOP	00700762 / $16.99
VOL. 100 – B.B. KING	00700466 / $16.99
VOL. 101 – SONGS FOR BEGINNERS	00701917 / $14.99
VOL. 102 – CLASSIC PUNK	00700769 / $14.99
VOL. 103 – SWITCHFOOT	00700773 / $16.99
VOL. 104 – DUANE ALLMAN	00700846 / $16.99
VOL. 105 – LATIN	00700939 / $16.99
VOL. 106 – WEEZER	00700958 / $14.99
VOL. 107 – CREAM	00701069 / $16.99
VOL. 108 – THE WHO	00701053 / $16.99
VOL. 109 – STEVE MILLER	00701054 / $19.99
VOL. 110 – SLIDE GUITAR HITS	00701055 / $16.99
VOL. 111 – JOHN MELLENCAMP	00701056 / $14.99
VOL. 112 – QUEEN	00701052 / $16.99
VOL. 113 – JIM CROCE	00701058 / $17.99
VOL. 114 – BON JOVI	00701060 / $16.99
VOL. 115 – JOHNNY CASH	00701070 / $16.99
VOL. 116 – THE VENTURES	00701124 / $16.99
VOL. 117 – BRAD PAISLEY	00701224 / $16.99
VOL. 118 – ERIC JOHNSON	00701353 / $16.99
VOL. 119 – AC/DC CLASSICS	00701356 / $17.99
VOL. 120 – PROGRESSIVE ROCK	00701457 / $14.99
VOL. 121 – U2	00701508 / $16.99
VOL. 122 – CROSBY, STILLS & NASH	00701610 / $16.99
VOL. 123 – LENNON & MCCARTNEY ACOUSTIC	00701614 / $16.99
VOL. 125 – JEFF BECK	00701687 / $16.99
VOL. 126 – BOB MARLEY	00701701 / $16.99
VOL. 127 – 1970S ROCK	00701739 / $16.99
VOL. 128 – 1960S ROCK	00701740 / $14.99
VOL. 129 – MEGADETH	00701741 / $17.99
VOL. 130 – IRON MAIDEN	00701742 / $17.99
VOL. 131 – 1990S ROCK	00701743 / $14.99
VOL. 132 – COUNTRY ROCK	00701757 / $15.99
VOL. 133 – TAYLOR SWIFT	00701894 / $16.99
VOL. 134 – AVENGED SEVENFOLD	00701906 / $16.99
VOL. 135 – MINOR BLUES	00151350 / $17.99
VOL. 136 – GUITAR THEMES	00701922 / $14.99
VOL. 137 – IRISH TUNES	00701966 / $15.99
VOL. 138 – BLUEGRASS CLASSICS	00701967 / $16.99
VOL. 139 – GARY MOORE	00702370 / $16.99
VOL. 140 – MORE STEVIE RAY VAUGHAN	00702396 / $17.99
VOL. 141 – ACOUSTIC HITS	00702401 / $16.99
VOL. 142 – GEORGE HARRISON	00237697 / $17.99

VOL. 143 – SLASH	00702425 / $19.99
VOL. 144 – DJANGO REINHARDT	00702531 / $16.99
VOL. 145 – DEF LEPPARD	00702532 / $17.99
VOL. 146 – ROBERT JOHNSON	00702533 / $16.99
VOL. 147 – SIMON & GARFUNKEL	14041591 / $16.99
VOL. 148 – BOB DYLAN	14041592 / $16.99
VOL. 149 – AC/DC HITS	14041593 / $17.99
VOL. 150 – ZAKK WYLDE	02501717 / $16.99
VOL. 151 – J.S. BACH	02501730 / $16.99
VOL. 152 – JOE BONAMASSA	02501751 / $19.99
VOL. 153 – RED HOT CHILI PEPPERS	00702990 / $19.99
VOL. 155 – ERIC CLAPTON – FROM THE ALBUM UNPLUGGED	00703085 / $16.99
VOL. 156 – SLAYER	00703770 / $17.99
VOL. 157 – FLEETWOOD MAC	00101382 / $16.99
VOL. 159 – WES MONTGOMERY	00102593 / $19.99
VOL. 160 – T-BONE WALKER	00102641 / $17.99
VOL. 161 – THE EAGLES – ACOUSTIC	00102659 / $17.99
VOL. 162 – THE EAGLES HITS	00102667 / $17.99
VOL. 163 – PANTERA	00103036 / $17.99
VOL. 164 – VAN HALEN 1986-1995	00110270 / $17.99
VOL. 165 – GREEN DAY	00210343 / $17.99
VOL. 166 – MODERN BLUES	00700764 / $16.99
VOL. 167 – DREAM THEATER	00111938 / $24.99
VOL. 168 – KISS	00113421 / $17.99
VOL. 169 – TAYLOR SWIFT	00115982 / $16.99
VOL. 170 – THREE DAYS GRACE	00117337 / $16.99
VOL. 171 – JAMES BROWN	00117420 / $16.99
VOL. 172 – THE DOOBIE BROTHERS	00119670 / $16.99
VOL. 173 – TRANS-SIBERIAN ORCHESTRA	00119907 / $19.99
VOL. 174 – SCORPIONS	00122119 / $16.99
VOL. 175 – MICHAEL SCHENKER	00122127 / $17.99
VOL. 176 – BLUES BREAKERS WITH JOHN MAYALL & ERIC CLAPTON	00122132 / $19.99
VOL. 177 – ALBERT KING	00123271 / $16.99
VOL. 178 – JASON MRAZ	00124165 / $17.99
VOL. 179 – RAMONES	00127073 / $16.99
VOL. 180 – BRUNO MARS	00129706 / $16.99
VOL. 181 – JACK JOHNSON	00129854 / $16.99
VOL. 182 – SOUNDGARDEN	00138161 / $17.99
VOL. 183 – BUDDY GUY	00138240 / $17.99
VOL. 184 – KENNY WAYNE SHEPHERD	00138258 / $17.99
VOL. 185 – JOE SATRIANI	00139457 / $17.99
VOL. 186 – GRATEFUL DEAD	00139459 / $17.99
VOL. 187 – JOHN DENVER	00140839 / $17.99
VOL. 188 – MÖTLEY CRUE	00141145 / $17.99
VOL. 189 – JOHN MAYER	00144350 / $17.99
VOL. 190 – DEEP PURPLE	00146152 / $17.99
VOL. 191 – PINK FLOYD CLASSICS	00146164 / $17.99
VOL. 192 – JUDAS PRIEST	00151352 / $17.99
VOL. 193 – STEVE VAI	00156028 / $19.99
VOL. 195 – METALLICA: 1983-1988	00234291 / $19.99
VOL. 196 – METALLICA: 1991-2016	00234292 / $19.99

Prices, contents, and availability subject to change without notice.

Complete song lists available online.

www.halleonard.com

0719
173